While a great deal of care has been taken to provide accurate and current information, the ideas, suggestions, general principles and conclusions presented in this book are subject to local, state and federal laws and regulations, court cases and any revisions of same. The reader is thus urged to consult legal counsel regarding any points of law—this publication should not be used as a substitute for competent legal advice.

© 1995 by Dearborn Financial Publishing, Inc.

Published by Dearborn Financial Publishing, Inc.

Printed in the United States of America.

95 96 97 10 9 8 7 6 5 4 3 2 1

Library of Congress Cataloging-in-Publication Data

Sambul, Nathan J.
    Top trader's guide to technical analysis : how to spot patterns
for big profits / Nathan J. Sambul.
      p. cm.
   Includes index.
   ISBN 0-7931-1415-2
   1. Stocks—Prices—Charts, diagrams, etc.   2. Futures—Charts,
diagrams, etc.   I. Title.   II. Title: Technical analysis.
   HG4638.S26   1995
332.63'222—dc20   94-46881
                                           CIP

DEDICATION

This one is for Harry Vogelman . . . a sage.

ACKNOWLEDGMENTS

The author would like to thank the following people who made this book possible:

Nick Van Nice, whose expertise gave me many insights and whose patience made putting this book together a lot easier

Joe Van Nice, a master of technical analysis

Dennis Blitz, the driving force on this project

Celia Sam, who makes certain things get done right

A special thanks to my wife, Nancy G. Sambul, who is the finest adviser and supporter a person could ever have.

The charts in this book have been supplied by Commodity Trend Service, Inc. (Palm Beach Gardens, Florida; 800-331-1069). They produce *Futures Charts,* a weekly compendium of agricultural and financial charts for professional traders.

CONTENTS

1 PRACTICE MAKES PERFECT

Your mother was correct: Practice makes perfect. That's the whole idea behind this easy-to-use, easy-to-understand workbook.

In the course of this book, you'll learn about the various technical analysis indicators that are available to you. But learning about them in the abstract is a whole other matter from actually finding them and highlighting them on real charts. What counts in successful futures trading is finding and using these indicators. This book will show you how to do that.

SMALL STEPS TO A LARGER GOAL

We have designed this book to deliver information in small, logical steps. Each pattern, each indicator, is explained and diagrammed. After you have mastered a pattern and understand what it looks like and how it can be used, you will have the opportunity to find and draw the pattern on an actual futures chart. In fact, you'll have multiple examples to practice on for each pattern and indicator.

Here is where practice makes perfect. You will have an opportunity to practice on the more than 100 examples in this book. Each example takes only a few seconds to spot and draw. The cumulative effect of this process is complete mastery of technical analysis.

There are two types of futures traders. First, some individual traders fly by the seat of their pants. Sure, they may be lucky for a period of time and score big on a number of trades. But, in the long run, because they never really understand the futures market, their success or failure is the luck of the draw.

The other type of futures trader is the professional. You do not have to have a large account to have a professional attitude. What is required is a willingness to study and apply the principles of sound futures trading. In this book, you will learn the techniques and skills that professional traders have used for years.

What is the ultimate goal? Year after year of successful, profitable trading. That is a major step, but you can accomplish this goal if you are willing to apply lessons you learn from this book.

AN INEXACT SCIENCE

As you go through the examples in this book, you'll notice that you will have to make reasonable assumptions. That is because technical analysis is an inexact science. Trend lines are never exactly straight. Volume may not peak on the day you expect it. Cycles may begin sooner or later than originally thought.

The point is: You have to be flexible with technical analysis. If you expect sharp peaks, straight lines and absolutely clear signals, you will be disappointed.

On the other hand, if you can see trends, if you are capable of projecting lines, if you understand the concept of momentum, then you'll have no problem with the examples in this book—and you'll have no problem analyzing charts on a day-to-day basis.

RULES TO FOLLOW

Investing in futures can be exhilarating, so it makes sense to use sound judgment when trading these instruments. Here are 11 rules to follow:

1. *Limit the total capital you have to invest.* Use about 30 percent for margin requirements. For example, if you have approximately $100,000, trade with only $30,000 and use the rest for reserve should the markets move against you.
2. *Diversify among markets.* Don't trade in just one or two markets. Diversify so that perhaps no more than 10 percent is in one market.
3. *Determine in advance the amount you are willing to risk.* Two percent is a reasonable number. So, if you have a $100,000 account, you should not risk more than $2,000 per trade.
4. *Do not trade impulsively.* Have a plan. Some of the most successful traders plan their trades when the market is closed, not when the numbers are flashing on their screens.
5. *Close out losing positions before winning ones.* To rephrase it, let profits run and cut losses short.
6. *Be mentally prepared to be in the minority.* Remember, the majority of inexperienced traders will be buying in an overbought zone and selling in an oversold zone.
7. *Chart from long-term monthly charts to weekly charts to daily charts.* Trade in the same direction.
8. *Stick to trading in the direction of the long-term trend.* (For more information, see Chapter 3.) If you are new to technical analysis, do not think you can always acquire during the accumulation stage or sell during the public participation phase.
9. *Choose a broker from a reputable firm that will help you.* Over time, you will have questions. A good broker will take the time to explain and educate. The broker who just wants to trade cares more about his or her pocket than yours.
10. *Start slow. Execute paper trades* (fictitious trades on paper that you follow, but never actually conduct). See how you perform. Modify your actions and experiment according to the principles you will learn in this book. In no time, you will develop a trading style of your own.
11. *Keep it simple.* Don't drive yourself crazy by applying every indicator to every market. There is a simple approach for everything. In time, you will develop a comfort level and know which indicators are most suited to your style of investing.

KEEP YOUR GOALS IN MIND

Financially, what do you want to achieve from trading? Additional income, funds for a trust account, the down payment on a house or a million dollars?

It is possible to generate major profits in a short period with commodity futures. Target a percentage goal that you want to achieve on an annual basis, and track your result.

By mastering technical analysis, you will be better prepared to review, decide and act with conviction. That is how you will reach your financial goal. As successful futures traders will tell you: Plan your trades and trade your plan— and success will likely follow!

2 | AN OVERVIEW OF FUTURES TRADING

Since the Chicago Board of Trade was created in 1848, futures trading has grown to encompass a wide variety of commodities and financial instruments. Today, there are nearly 40 futures exchanges worldwide—12 in the United States—where traders and hedgers buy and sell futures contracts in such items as corn, feeder cattle, deutsche mark, gold, heating oil and Treasury bills.

CASH MARKET VERSUS FUTURES MARKET

Commodities can be purchased or sold in either the cash or futures market. These are two separate but related markets.

In the *cash market,* also known as the *actual* or *spot market,* commodities are transacted on a negotiated basis. In the majority of instances, the contract calls for the actual transfer of the commodity. The contract may specify immediate delivery or a time set in the future. The latter is referred to as *forward delivery.*

Cash prices respond to supply and demand factors. If there is an abundant supply of a particular commodity, its cash price will fall. On the other hand, if there is a shortage of a commodity, the people who need it (e.g., manufacturers, processors and distributors) will bid up the cash price. Supply and demand can also be seasonally related. Jewelers need gold and silver in September so that they can prepare their holiday inventory. Consequently, gold and silver prices generally rise after Labor Day.

Cash prices can be found in most major newspapers. They are divided into categories: grains and oilseeds; livestock and meat; food and fiber; metals and petroleum; interest rate; currency; index; and other futures. Examples of cash and future prices are shown in Figures 2.1 and 2.2.

FIGURE 2.1   Sample Cash Prices

Wednesday, November 3, 1993.
(Closing Market Quotations)

	Wed.	Tues.	Yr. Ago
Coffee Colombian NY lb	.83	.84½	.71
Copper Scrap No. 2 wire NY lb	.55½	.55¼	.85½
Soybean Oil crude Decatur lb	.2348	.2363	.1918
Wheat No. 2 KC bu	3.40¾	3.40¾	3.66¼

How to read this chart: On Wednesday, Colombian coffee sold in New York at a wholesale price of 83¢ per pound. On Tuesday, the day before, a pound sold for 84½¢ a pound. The current price is higher than it was a year ago when a pound sold for 71¢.

In the *futures* market, standardized contracts, not the actual commodities, are bought and sold. The terms of futures contracts specify:

■ Quantity of the commodity
■ Quality of the commodity
■ Date when delivery is to be made
■ Location at which delivery is to be made

In over 99 percent of all cases, the commodity is never delivered. Buyers offset their positions by selling their contracts before delivery month, and sellers offset their positions by purchasing contracts.

FIGURE 2.2   **Sample Futures Prices**

Corn (CBT) 5,000 bu.; cents per bu.

	Open	High	Low	Settle	Change	Lifetime High	Low	Open Interest
Dec	259	261¾	258	260¾	+3	268½	225¼	152,458
Mar94	266¾	269¾	265	268¾	+3	269¾	232¾	85,307

Est vol 75,000; vol Tues 71,553; open int 311,375, +6476

Next to the commodity (corn) is the exchange on which it is traded (the Chicago Board of Trade). Each contract consists of 5,000 bushels and it is quoted in cents per bushel (261¾ = $2.61¾ per bushel).

The first column gives the delivery month. The second indicates where the contract opened. The next two columns show the high and low of the day's trading range. The fifth column is the settlement price. Change represents the difference from the previous day's settlement price. Lifetime high and low details the highest and lowest prices for the contract since it began trading. Open interest is the number of open contracts for each delivery month.

The bottom line contains the cumulative volume and open interest for that particular commodity. In this example, open interest increased by 6,476 contracts from the previous trading session.

WHO ARE THE PLAYERS?

Traders generally fall into one of three categories:

1. *Hedger.* A hedger is an individual who uses the futures market for price insurance—in essence, to protect his or her cash position.

A classic example is the Kansas farmer who likes the current price of wheat at $3.50 a bushel and would like to lock it in. The farmer sells wheat futures. Six months later, when the grain is ready for harvest, it is selling at a lower price and the farmer will suffer a loss on the spot market. Fortunately, the farmer can buy back the futures contracts at a lower price and realize a gain. The gain made in the futures market par-

tially offsets the loss in the cash market, and the farmer still ends up
with approximately $3.50 a bushel.

2. *Speculator.* A speculator is a trader who attempts to profit by correctly
anticipating price movements. Speculators do not want to take delivery
of the commodity. They add liquidity to the market as they increase the
number of contracts bought and sold. Through the leveraging effect of
margin, speculators can see substantial gains or losses when a commodity moves in one direction or another.

As a case in point, a speculator who believes oil is going up in price in
the next few weeks can purchase a crude oil contract at $21.25 a barrel.
If oil does go up, say to $21.75, that 50-cent rise, at 1,000 barrels per
contract, represents a $500 gain. Since the speculator's original margin
was $2,100, the $500 gain represents a 24 percent return on investment
in a matter of weeks. Very few investments can move that far, that fast.

3. *Floor trader.* This individual is an exchange member who is physically
present on the exchange floor and who executes orders in the trading
pit. A floor trader who trades for his or her own account is generally
known as a *local.* One who executes trades for others is known as a
floor broker.

NET-SUM-ZERO: A WINNER FOR EVERY LOSER

It is important to understand that futures trading is a net-sum-zero game. For
every winner there is a loser on every single trade. Without a disciplined
approach to futures trading, you could find yourself funding someone else's
pocket—and the money will come from yours.

Futures trading is not like the stock market, where an investor could purchase
XYZ common stock at $20 a share, sell it at $30; the next investor can ride it
from $30 to $40 a share and sell it to another investor; and that one can hold it
to $60 a share—three investors, all of whom made money.

In futures trading, you make or lose money on every single trade. The rule of
thumb is to cut your losses short and let your profitable trades run.

MARGIN

An investor gives a broker an order to buy or sell a contract, depending on which way the investor believes the market is heading. When the order is filled, all orders go into a pool at the exchange. It is the exchange's responsibility to pair all buyers and sellers, which it does in an anonymous fashion. A *futures contract* is, therefore, a pair of promises—one to deliver the underlying commodity and the other to pay for it.

The exchange requires brokerage firms to collect from investors good faith deposits on their transactions. An investor's deposit is called *margin*. As opposed to margin in equity transactions, the balance of the value of the futures contract is not borrowed. Therefore, no loan interest is paid by the contract holder.

The purpose of margin is to ensure that the buyer and seller will perform as expected (i.e., one will deliver and the other will accept and pay). The sum of money that an investor is required to deposit is called *original margin* or *initial margin*.

The amount that needs to be deposited initially is determined by the exchange on which the contract is traded and varies according to price level, volatility and other factors. Generally, original margin ranges from 2 percent to 10 percent of the value of the contract. Margin requirements can change a few times a year or even weekly or daily depending on the price movement of the underlying commodity. Although the exchanges set the initial margin, each member firm of the exchange may require higher levels, known as *house margin requirements*.

After a position is established, the price of the futures contract will increase or decrease depending on market action. At the end of every business day, money is credited to or debited from an account based on the amount that the contract has moved during the day. This daily activity is known as *marking to the market*. If a price movement is adverse to a client's position, the original margin that was deposited may be reduced or depleted.

Once the margin is reduced to a certain level, known as the *maintenance margin,* the member firm must request additional funds. This is known as *variation margin call* or *maintenance margin call*. As an example, if an exchange set its maintenance margin requirement at 75 percent, a customer would receive a variation margin call if the individual's account dropped below 75 percent of the original requirement. The variation margin call would restore the account to the full original margin and not the lower amount of the maintenance margin. Variation margin calls can be met either by depositing additional funds or by liquidating or reducing a position.

Of course, when the market moves in favor of the investor and the account is marked to the market, the individual will have increased value in his or her account. This is known as an increase in the *equity* in the account. This additional value may be withdrawn as cash or may be used for other trading (e.g., the purchase of additional contracts). This increase in equity gives the investor an opportunity to take on new positions without putting up additional funds. A note of caution, though: If the market moves against the investor, the individual may have a larger variation margin call.

How Successful Professionals Analyze the Market

Successful professionals and intelligent investors who trade in futures use research to help them determine the direction of the market and to forecast prices. Through their efforts, investors analyze whether to buy, sell or stay out of the market for a period.

MARKET ANALYSIS

Market research generally falls into one of two camps: *fundamental analysis* and *technical analysis*. Individual investors may use both; however, more often than not, they will gravitate to one approach over another.

Fundamental Analysis

Fundamental analysis is based on the traditional study of supply and demand. A supply-and-demand philosophy assumes that a scarcity of a commodity should result in a higher average price level. After examining all the factors, the fundamentalist assumes a market position.

In the financial futures markets, factors such as government policy, trade deficits, changes in the money supply, international developments and the performance of the equity markets are studied and considered when conducting fundamental analysis.

In the agricultural futures markets, fundamentalists study weather patterns, crop conditions, planted acres and many other components.

Fundamental analysis tends to be long-term in nature. It is also closely tied with seasonal trends. There are some inherent weaknesses to this approach. Fundamental analysis cannot review and consider all the many variables that influence price. As a result, surprise factors can often disrupt the analysis process. In addition, since futures markets are very price-efficient, prices tend to discount fundamental analysis and information as quickly as it becomes known.

Technical Analysis

Technical analysis is the study of market action. Its aim is to anticipate future price trends and it does so primarily through the use of charts.

The basis of the technical analysis philosophy is the belief that all factors influencing market price action are quickly reflected in market activity. The impact of these factors will quickly show up in some form of price movement. It follows, therefore, that a study of price action is all that is required.

Technical analysis can accomplish a number of goals. It can provide price forecasting. Since charting is highly suited for rapid decisions, it is an excellent means of determining market timing—when to enter or exit a position.

Generally, chartists do not concern themselves with the reasons why prices rise or fall. If prices are rising, for whatever reason, technicians conclude that the fundamentals must be bullish. If prices fall, the fundamentals must be bearish. Technicians are indirectly studying fundamentals.

Recognize that charts do not cause the markets to go up or down. They simply reflect the bullish or bearish psychology of the market. By studying charts and a host of supporting technical indicators, the chartist lets the market tell him or her which way prices are most likely to go. In short, the chartist consults the market on the market, not the opinion of others.

THE CORE OF TECHNICAL ANALYSIS

To truly understand the philosophy of technical analysis, you need to understand three core concepts, which are the basis by which all technical analysis is conducted:

1. Market action reflects all information.
2. Prices move in trends.
3. Everything repeats.

Market Action Reflects All Information

Information such as crop forecasts, weather conditions, OPEC meetings, mergers and announcements by the Federal Reserve impact various markets. Prices may go up or down as a result of the interpretation of these and other factors.

To the technician, or chartist, the market absorbs that information, which is then reflected in current prices. By the time an investor hears the news of a major bit of information, the market has already acted on it. If an investor tries to figure out the impact of every ounce of information, that individual would play a catch-up game forever—and probably lose.

The technician is not concerned with the reasons for a price change. The technician accepts the change and is more interested in the direction of the price change, than in the rationale behind it. The technician leaves the rationale to the fundamental analyst.

Prices Move in Trends

Prices can move up, down or sideways. The important thing to note is that they move in a direction until something changes the direction. Prices do not change by themselves. Outside information and influences, which are quickly absorbed into market action, will change a price trend. And that trend will remain in effect until more economic news or other influences appear. It is this momentum of trends that allows for technical forecasting—a key strength of charting.

Everything Repeats

It is sometimes difficult to accept that humans are so predictable, but it's true. A company issues good news and everyone jumps on the bandwagon and buys the stock and the option. The Governors of the Federal Reserve Bank announce dire news about rising inflation and everyone sells their bonds. Patterns start to emerge and these patterns are predictable. In a way, charting and the study of human psychology go hand in hand. Price patterns repeat because human behavior repeats.

THE DOW THEORY—THE CORNERSTONE OF TECHNICAL ANALYSIS

The foundation of technical analysis is hundreds of years old. The Japanese are regarded as the true pioneers of technical analysis. Back in the mid-1700s, Japanese businessmen charted the price of what we now would call "rice futures" in order to forecast the price of the rice market. One family in particular—the Homma family, who were rice merchants—developed what has evolved as the Japanese method of charting. Today, this method is used worldwide and generally is referred to as *candlestick charting.*

Modern technical analysis has had a number of major contributors to the field. Prominent among them was Charles H. Dow, cofounder of Dow Jones & Co., publishers of the *Wall Street Journal.*

While Charles Dow never wrote a book on his theory, he did write a series of editorials, which became the basis for the Dow theory. Although he dealt with the averages, like the industrials and transportation, his ideas had far wider applicability. Following are some of his basic rules.

The Averages Discount Everything

The view that the averages discount everything is already a familiar concept, since it is the same as "market action reflects all information." The daily closing prices of the Dow Jones Industrial Average, the Standard & Poor's 500 Stock Index and the Russell 2,000 all reflect the aggregate judgment of every market participant.

The Market Has Three Trends

An *uptrend* is a pattern of rising peaks and valleys, with each successive high and low being higher than the previous respective peak or valley. Conversely, a *downtrend* consists of successively lower highs and lower lows.

Charles Dow divided trends into three different categories, illustrated in Figure 3.1.

FIGURE 3.1   Market Trends

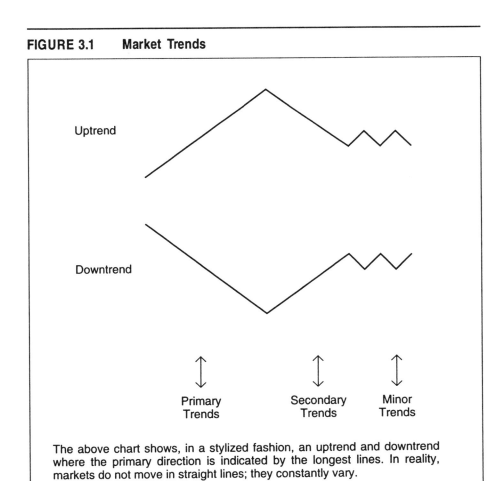

The above chart shows, in a stylized fashion, an uptrend and downtrend where the primary direction is indicated by the longest lines. In reality, markets do not move in straight lines; they constantly vary.

Primary Trends

A *primary trend* or *major trend* can last from one to several years in duration. A primary trend can be bullish or bearish in nature.

Secondary Trends

A *secondary trend* or *intermediate trend* represents a correction in the primary trend. As corrections, they travel in an opposite direction from a major trend. Secondary trends last from a few weeks to several months and normally retrace one-third to two-thirds of the previous trend.

Minor Trends

A *minor trend* consists of minor movements. They can run as short as a few hours or as long as three weeks and they can be found in both primary and secondary trends.

Primary Trends Have Three Phases

Within a primary or major trend, Dow and other market analysts recognized three distinct phases, illustrated in Figure 3.2.

Accumulation Stage

The first phase is called the *accumulation stage,* in which the smart money assumes a position. Investors have discounted all the prior bad economic news and see an opportunity ahead.

Trend-Following Stage

The second phase is the *trend-following stage*. Prices tend to increase rapidly. In the stock market, you'll see even lesser quality issues start moving up in price as more and more investors get caught up in the momentum.

Public Participation Stage

The last phase is the *public participation stage.* By now, the general press is carrying banner headlines—a particular commodity is hot or certain stocks and options are Wall Street favorites. In a bull market, speculation volume

FIGURE 3.2   Three Phases of a Primary Trend

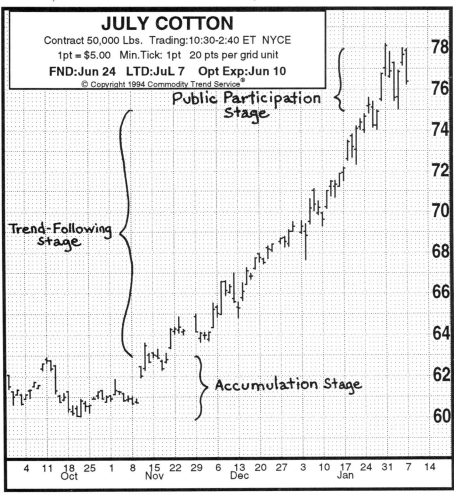

increases. Of course, that is when the smart money sells off their positions—also referred to as *distribution*.

Confirmations and Divergences

Charles Dow recommended looking for *confirmations* and *divergences* in the averages and in price/volume relationships. If prices moved up rapidly along with heavy volume, that would be a confirming indicator. On the other hand, if prices increased, but volume slacked off, that divergence could signal a weakening position. In essence, market analysts prefer seeing the Dow Jones Industrial Average and the S&P 500 Stock Index, for example, move in tandem. When they start to diverge, that is the time to be cautious.

It is important to remember that no one indicator can be the be-all-and-end-all of technical analysis. Multiple indicators must be used together to confirm a buy or sell signal.

Trend Reversal

Finally, Charles Dow felt that a trend continues until it gives a signal that it has reversed. What are some of those signals? Well, a change in resistance levels, moving averages and stochastics are just a few. This book will explain how to read those signals later on, but for now remember this important point: *Signals are not always clear-cut.* You get better and better spotting trends the more you work at it, the more charting you do and by using charts that are easy to read and understand.

4 | THE BASICS OF CHARTING: PRICE AND TIME

To use charts successfully, you must first understand the components of charting. Charts can take many forms and reflect different periods. This chapter will familiarize you with the basics of charting.

CHART COMPONENTS

All charts have two elements in common: price and time.

Value of Different Types of Charts

Bar Charts

There are numerous ways of graphing price action during a given period; however, the most common is the bar chart, as shown in Figure 4.1. Each bar can represent a month, a week, a day or even a 30- or 60-minute time span.

Using gold as an example, the top of the bar in Figure 4.1 is the high price during a period of time; in this case, $405.30 per troy ounce. The bottom of the vertical bar is the low price traded—$397.80.

FIGURE 4.1   Sample Bar Chart Showing Price Action for a Given
                Time Period

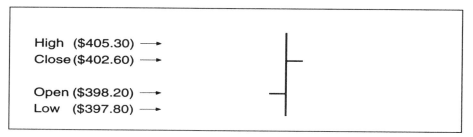

There are two horizontal tick marks. The one on the left is the opening price during that month, week, day or multiminute interval. The opening in Figure 4.1 is $398.20. The tick mark on the right is the closing price—$402.60.

In this example, the opening price was below the closing price; however, in reality, any number of combinations can exist—the opening and close can be at the same price, the opening can be the high of the day, the close could be the high of the day and so on.

The prices printed in the margins of a chart represent the current trading range of the commodity. In the example shown in Figure 4.2, the S&P 500 traded from approximately 180 to 470.

Monthly Charts

These charts can go back 20 to 40 years. Because "everything repeats," these monthly charts give an excellent macro, long-term perspective. Trends are easier to define when examining monthly charts. For example, the overall trend of the S&P 500 has been upward. (See Figure 4.2.)

Weekly Charts

Weekly charts go back three or more years. After examining the macro monthly view, you can use weekly charts to verify whether a trend is continuing. Despite its ups and downs, we do see an upward slope in the S&P 500 as shown in the weekly chart of Figure 4.3.

Daily Charts

While weekly charts can confirm trends, it is very difficult to trade using weekly charts, because the time frame is too broad. You need a more micro view. That is the benefit of a daily chart. Daily charts go back six or seven months. In Figure 4.4, we see the S&P 500 trading in a range from approximately 445 to 475.

FIGURE 4.2   Sample Monthly Chart

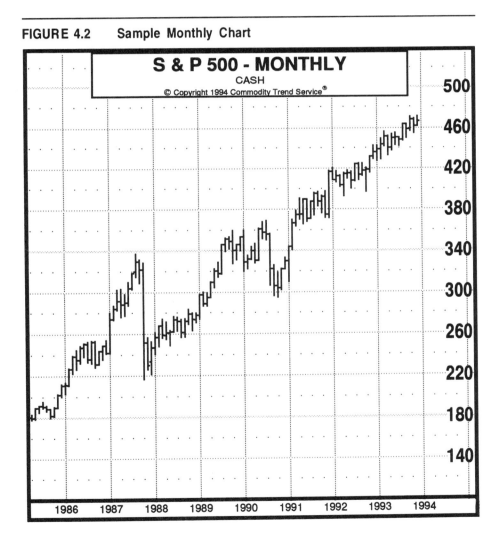

S & P 500 - MONTHLY
CASH
© Copyright 1994 Commodity Trend Service®

FIGURE 4.3   Sample Weekly Chart

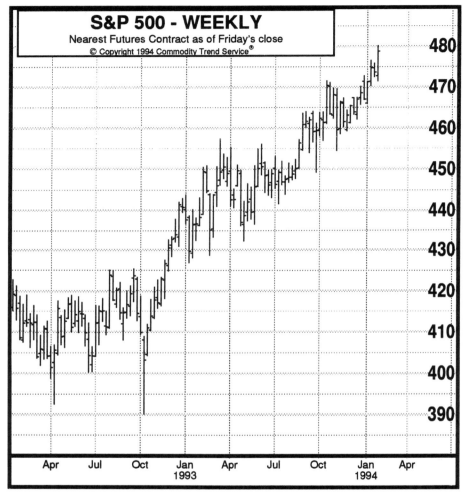

FIGURE 4.4   Sample Daily Chart

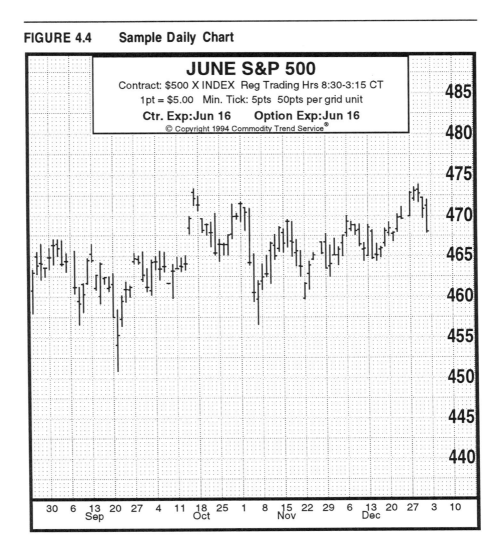

FUTURES CHARTS

As you examine the charts provided by Commodity Trend Service's Futures Charts, you will see a number of boxes that present detailed information about the contract under consideration. Figures 4.5 and 4.6 are keys to these boxes.

FIGURE 4.5   Contract Specification Box

MARCH 94 HIGH GRADE COPPER
Contract 25,000 Lbs. Trading: 9:25-2:00 EST COMEX
1 pt=$2.50 Min. Tick: 5pts 20pts per grid unit
FND:Feb 28 LTD:Mar 29 Opt Exp:Feb 23

Line #1: This futures contract is for High Grade Copper with delivery set for March 1994.

Line #2: Each contract consists of 25,000 pounds of high grade copper; therefore, a one-cent move in copper translates to a $250 move in the contract price. The contract trades on the Commodity Exchange, in New York, every business day from 9:25 A.M. to 2:00 P.M., eastern standard time.

Line #3: On the floor of the Commodity Exchange, the price of high grade copper moves in point increments, with each point equaling $2.50 (or 1/10th of a cent per pound). However, the minimum "tick" (price change) is 5 points or $12.50 (½¢ per pound). On the chart in Commodity Trend Service's *Futures Charts,* each grid unit represents 20 points or $50.00 (20¢ per pound).

Line #4: FND refers to first notice day—the first day that clients who are short the position may notify their brokers that they intend to deliver the commodity. In all futures markets, the time of delivery is at the option of the short. This is for those contracts that have not been offset and remain open at the end of the delivery period, which must be fulfilled by physical delivery. LTD refers to the last trading day of the contract. Opt. Exp. refers to the option expiration date of the option on high grade copper.

FIGURE 4.6   Price Information Box

Date	Open	High	Low	Close
11/01	7360	7375	**7305**	7365
11/02	7410	7475	7410	7455
11/03	7485	7490	7420	7425
11/04	7460	7515	7455	7505
11/05	7550	**7620**	7505	7540

In this example from March 94 High Grade Copper, the price information box gives you the open, high, low and closing prices of the past five trading sessions (in this case, the first week in November). The numbers that are boxed are the high and low figures for the week. The low was 73.05¢ per pound. The high was 76.20¢ per pound.

<table>
<tr><td>

5

</td><td>

IT ALL STARTS WITH TREND LINES

</td></tr>
</table>

Technical analysis would be very easy if markets moved in straight lines, but they don't! Over time, prices move up, down and sideways. The initial task for the professional trader is to determine the direction of the primary trend. This chapter will help you focus on spotting and drawing primary trends the way the professionals do.

TREND LINES

Following are a few simple thoughts and suggestions on drawing trend lines.

Connect the Points

As your geometry teacher taught you in high school, you need only two points to draw a line. The same holds true in technical analysis. Start with two points. Finding a third point confirms the validity of the trend line.

Extend Your Lines

Investors use technical analysis for its predictive qualities. If you draw your lines just between two points, all you are doing is plotting the past. Extend your lines beyond the two points. That way, you will concentrate on where the market is heading and you will be more attuned to corrective moves that run counter to the trend lines.

Adjust Trend Lines

Start drawing trend lines in pencil. It's not unusual to draw two or three lines as a trend develops. Once you are more confident that you have determined the primary trend, you can move to ink.

Look for Major Patterns

You will find, over and over, that technical analysis is an inexact science, especially when it comes to drawing trend lines, crossover points, cycles and so on. There will always be the occasional blips that will cross your lines and confuse you if you're not careful. Ignore them. Look for the major pattern.

UPTRENDS

An *uptrend* consists of a series of higher highs and higher lows, where each peak and valley is higher than the one preceding it. To plot an uptrend, draw your line connecting successive lows, where the second low is higher than the first.

FIGURE 5.1   Example of an Uptrend

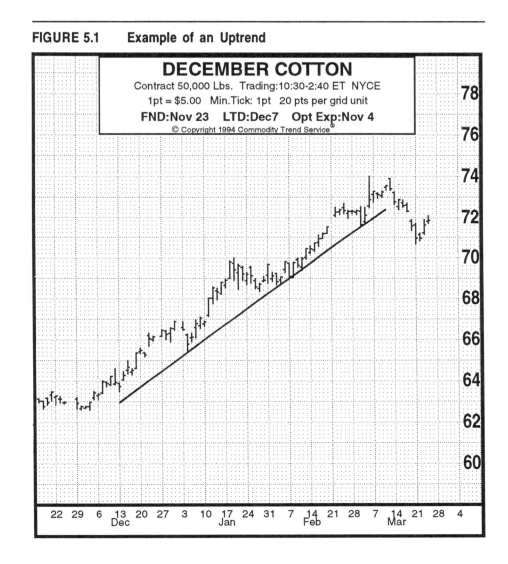

DECEMBER COTTON

Contract 50,000 Lbs. Trading:10:30-2:40 ET NYCE

1pt = $5.00   Min.Tick: 1pt   20 pts per grid unit

FND:Nov 23   LTD:Dec7   Opt Exp:Nov 4

© Copyright 1994 Commodity Trend Service®

YOU
CAN
DO IT

Figures 5.2 and 5.4 contain uptrending patterns. Using a pencil and ruler, plot them on the page. Remember to connect successive lows. Extend the lines. Now is the time to get comfortable with the drawing process. You'll find the solutions in Figures 5.3 and 5.5. Remember, practice makes perfect, so start drawing now.

FIGURE 5.2   **YOU CAN DO IT**
Chart an Uptrend
Number 1

FIGURE 5.3   **ANSWER**
Chart an Uptrend
Number 1

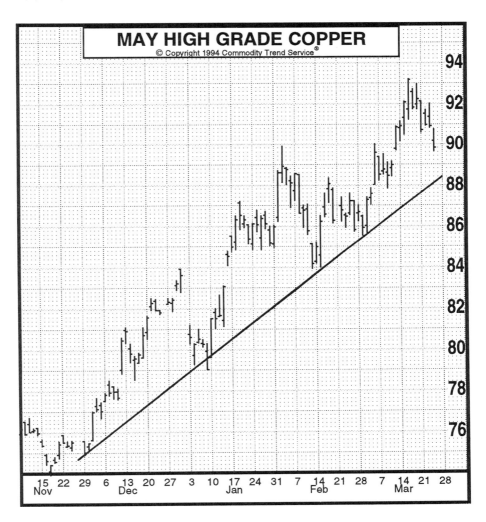

FIGURE 5.4   **YOU CAN DO IT**
Chart an Uptrend
Number 2

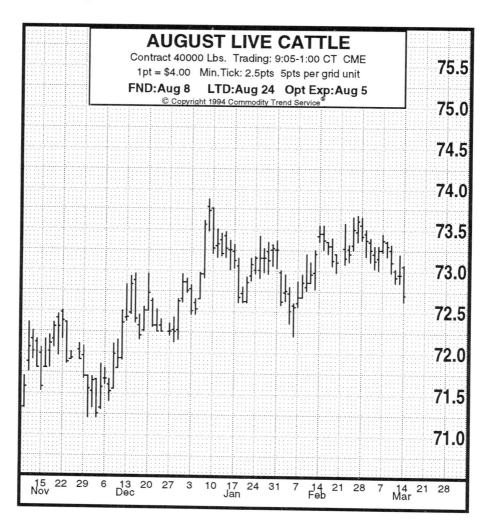

AUGUST LIVE CATTLE
Contract 40000 Lbs. Trading: 9:05-1:00 CT CME
1pt = $4.00 Min.Tick: 2.5pts 5pts per grid unit
FND:Aug 8   LTD:Aug 24   Opt Exp:Aug 5
© Copyright 1994 Commodity Trend Service®

FIGURE 5.5   ANSWER
Chart an Uptrend
Number 2

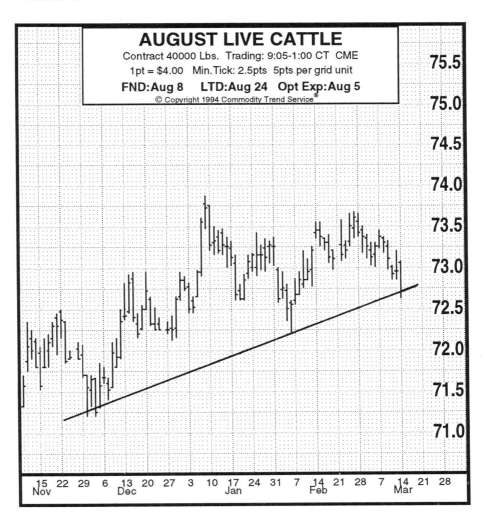

AUGUST LIVE CATTLE
Contract 40000 Lbs. Trading: 9:05-1:00 CT CME
1pt = $4.00   Min.Tick: 2.5pts 5pts per grid unit
FND:Aug 8   LTD:Aug 24   Opt Exp:Aug 5
© Copyright 1994 Commodity Trend Service®

DOWNTRENDS

A *downtrend* consists of a series of descending highs and lows, where each peak and valley is lower than the one preceding it. To plot a downtrend, draw your line connecting successive highs, where the second high is lower than the first. For examples of downtrends, see Figures 5.6 and 5.7.

FIGURE 5.6   Downtrend: Example #1

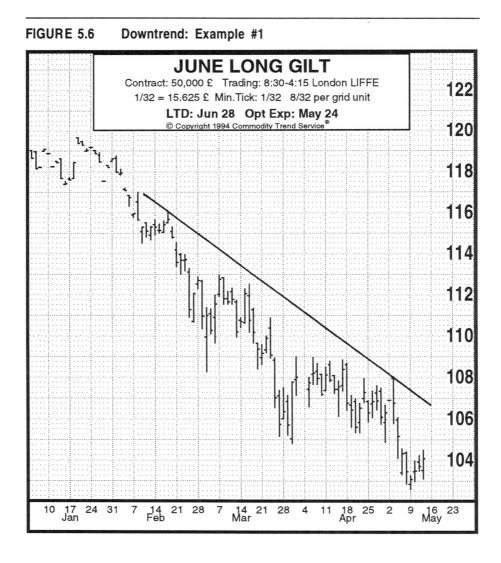

JUNE LONG GILT
Contract: 50,000 £   Trading: 8:30-4:15 London LIFFE
1/32 = 15.625 £ Min.Tick: 1/32   8/32 per grid unit
LTD: Jun 28   Opt Exp: May 24
© Copyright 1994 Commodity Trend Service®

Because downtrends and uptrends can vary widely, it is perfectly acceptable to have more than one trend line in a chart.

FIGURE 5.7   Downtrend: Example #2

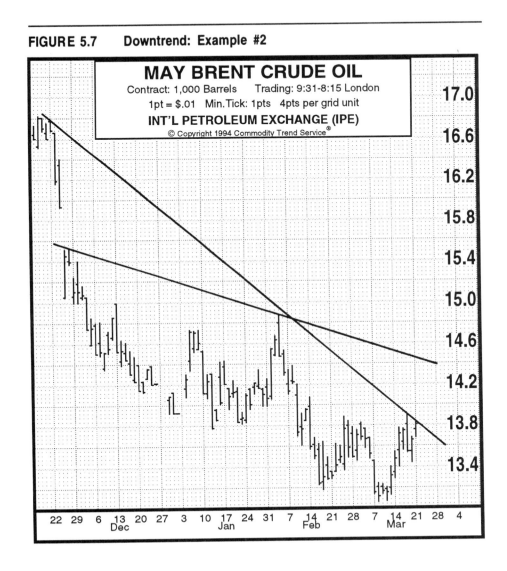

MAY BRENT CRUDE OIL
Contract: 1,000 Barrels   Trading: 9:31-8:15 London
1pt = $.01   Min.Tick: 1pts   4pts per grid unit
INT'L PETROLEUM EXCHANGE (IPE)
© Copyright 1994 Commodity Trend Service®

YOU
CAN
DO IT

Figures 5.8 and 5.10 are your chances to practice drawing downtrend lines. You will find the answers in Figures 5.9 and 5.11. Here you are going to connect successive peaks.

FIGURE 5.8   **YOU CAN DO IT**
Chart a Downtrend
Number 1

FIGURE 5.9   **ANSWER**
Downtrend
Number 1

FIGURE 5.10   YOU CAN DO IT
Chart a Downtrend
Number 2

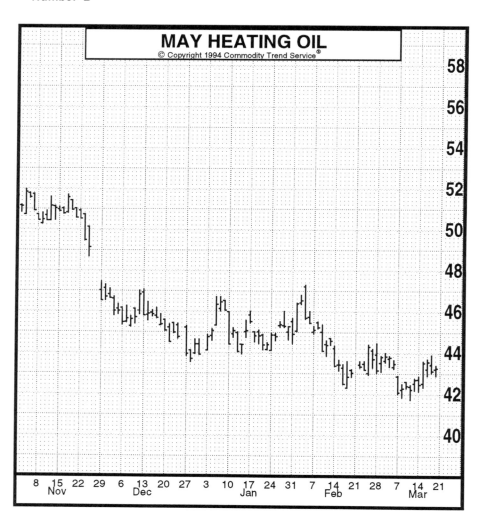

FIGURE 5.11 **ANSWER**
Downtrend
Number 2

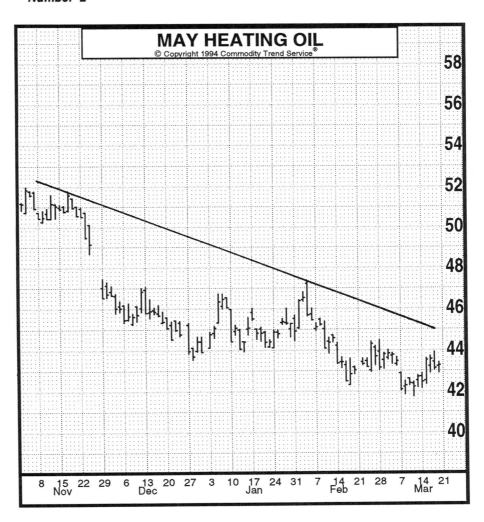

CHANNELS

When prices fluctuate within a discernible pattern that can be drawn by two parallel lines, we say that a *channel* is formed. A channel can move upward, downward or sideways. A sideways trend, illustrated in Figure 5.12, can be referred to as *trendless* or as a *congestion area*.

The two parallel lines can be defined as support and resistance lines. A *support* line (the lower line) occurs where there is sufficient buying interest to overcome any selling pressure. When prices move to a *resistance* level (the higher line), there are more sellers than buyers and prices retreat.

What's the logic behind support and resistance lines? Well, imagine a lot of people buying silver at $4.25 only to see the price drop instead of rise. As the price returns to $4.25, human nature being what it is, these people would like to break even—so they sell at $4.25. As long as there is selling pressure at $4.25, you'll find a resistance level there.

At some point, a channel will be broken. If prices move up, resistance becomes support. If prices move down, support becomes resistance. How far will prices move? You can plot the distance equal to the width of the old channel as shown in Figure 5.13. That is a reasonable price target for an anticipated price move, which, as you can see, did occur.

FIGURE 5.12 Example of a Sideways Channel

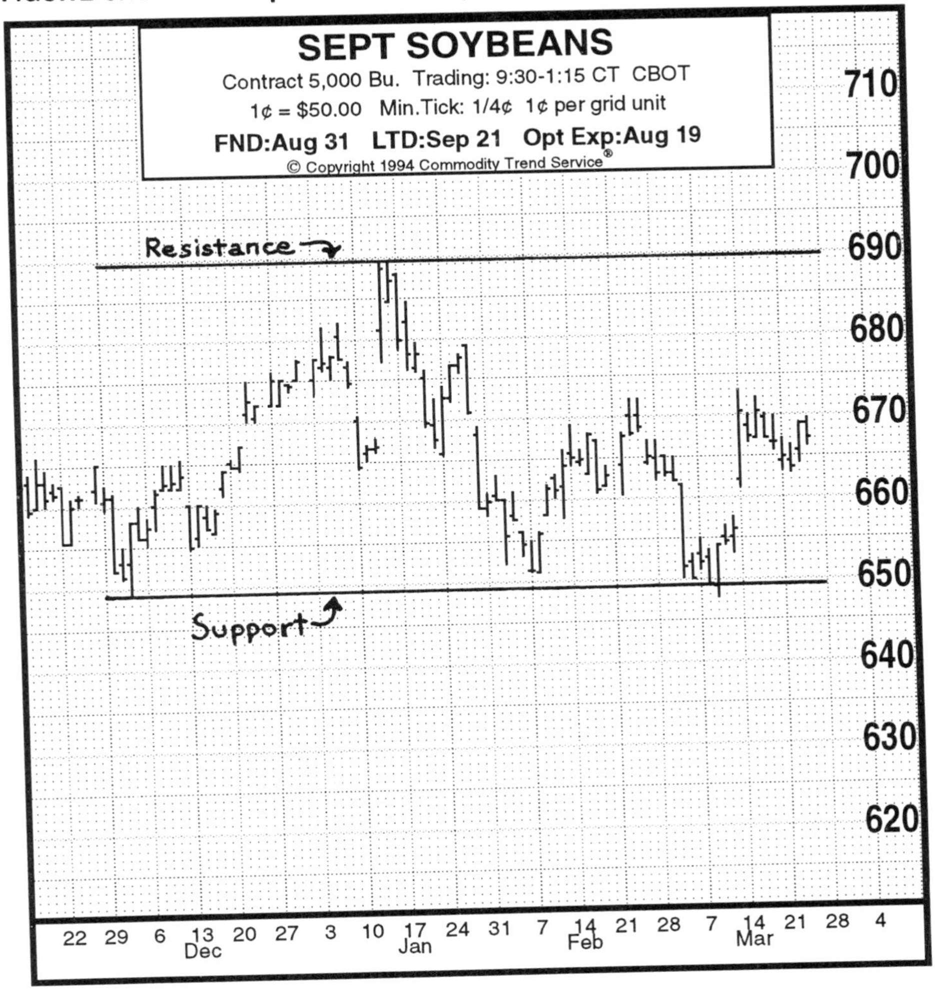
SEPT SOYBEANS
Contract 5,000 Bu. Trading: 9:30-1:15 CT CBOT
1¢ = $50.00 Min.Tick: 1/4¢ 1¢ per grid unit
FND:Aug 31 LTD:Sep 21 Opt Exp:Aug 19
© Copyright 1994 Commodity Trend Service®
Resistance
Support
710
700
690
680
670
660
650
640
630
620
22 29 6 13 20 27 3 10 17 24 31 7 14 21 28 7 14 21 28 4
Dec
Jan
Feb
Mar

FIGURE 5.13   Support, Resistance and Target Price

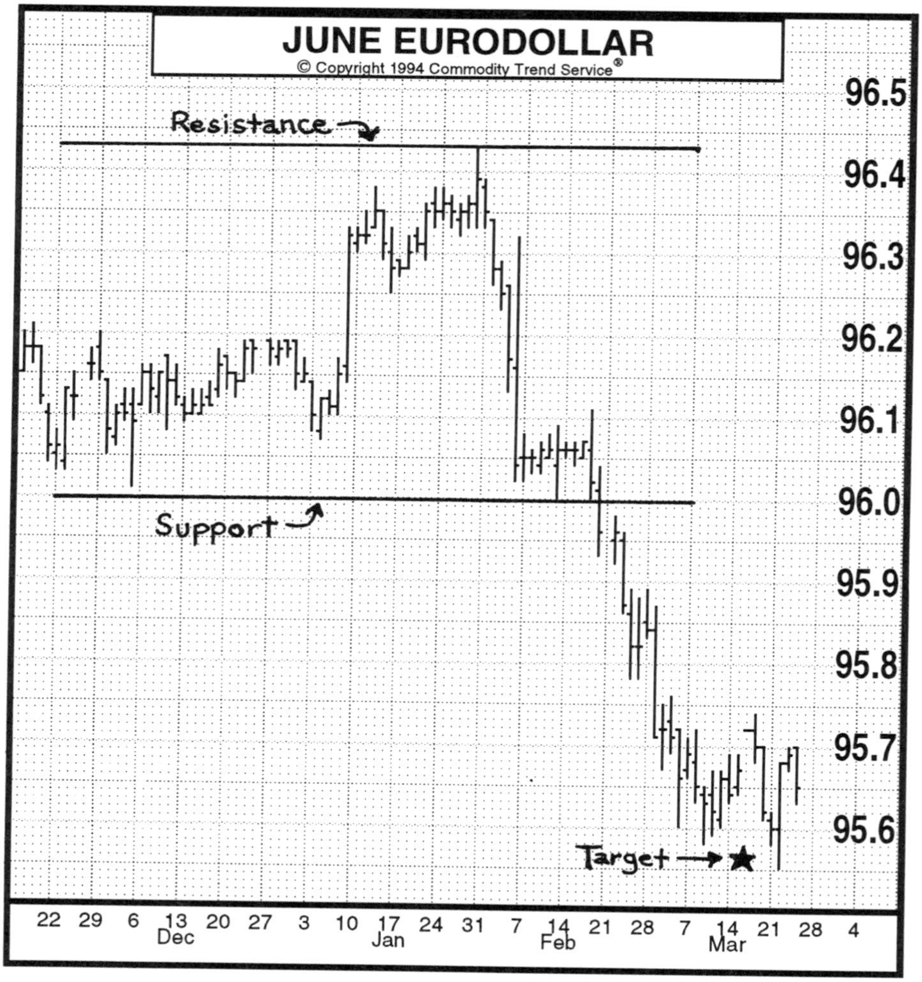

In Figures 5.14 and 5.16, you cannot only draw channels, but also estimate a future target price. Use the width of your channel as an estimate. Label your support and resistance lines, as well as your target level. Answers are shown in Figures 5.15 and 5.17.

FIGURE 5.14 **YOU CAN DO IT**
Chart a Channel
Number 1

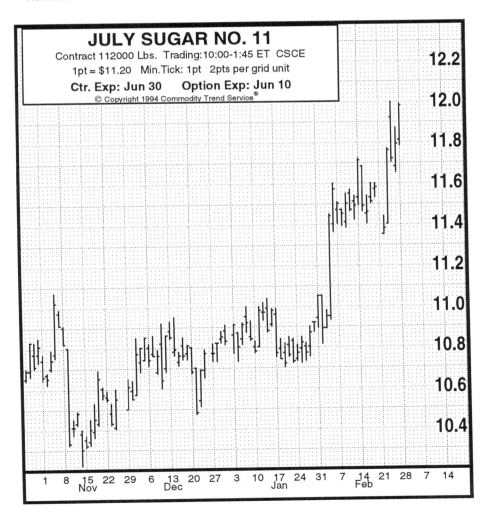

FIGURE 5.15   **ANSWER**
Channel
Number 1

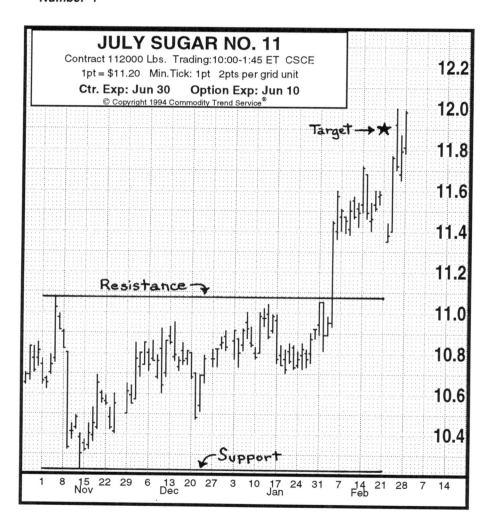

FIGURE 5.16 **YOU CAN DO IT**
Chart a Channel
Number 2

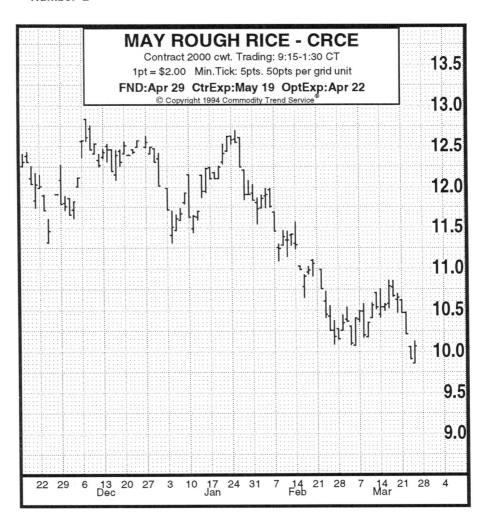

MAY ROUGH RICE - CRCE
Contract 2000 cwt. Trading: 9:15-1:30 CT
1pt = $2.00 Min.Tick: 5pts. 50pts per grid unit
FND:Apr 29 CtrExp:May 19 OptExp:Apr 22
© Copyright 1994 Commodity Trend Service®

FIGURE 5.17   **ANSWER**
Channel
Number 2

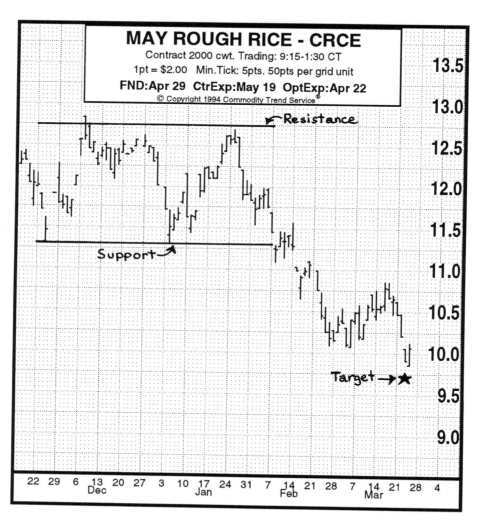

MAY ROUGH RICE - CRCE
Contract 2000 cwt. Trading: 9:15-1:30 CT
1pt = $2.00   Min.Tick: 5pts. 50pts per grid unit
FND:Apr 29 CtrExp:May 19 OptExp:Apr 22
© Copyright 1994 Commodity Trend Service®

6

LOOKING AT THE NUMBERS— VOLUME AND OPEN INTEREST

Imagine that you are packing for a camping exposition. You look at your map, where you see a body of water, but you don't know if it is a stream or a raging river. It certainly would be helpful to know which it is so you can plan your trip accordingly.

The same is true in technical analysis. In the world of charting, if price represents movement, volume and open interest represent pressure or strength. This chapter will help you "read the map" so you can forge across the terrain.

VOLUME

Volume represents the total number of contracts traded during the day. It is the total number of buys or sells, but not of both. You don't add them together, because that would double the volume.

The volume is drawn as a vertical bar at the bottom of the chart under that day's price bar. The higher the line, the larger the volume for that period. Conversely, a smaller line represents lighter volume.

Rules of Thumb

■ As a rule of thumb, *volume should increase in the direction of the existing price trend,* as shown in Figure 6.1. If a trend slopes upward, volume gets larger. The same holds true if a trend line is down. You still want to see increasing volume.

The logic is simple. When you see increasing volume, you have confirmation that strong buying or selling is behind the trend. If, on the other hand, prices are increasing and you notice a declining volume, then you have found a divergence. That indicator may mean that the uptrend is running out of steam and may be due for a correction.

One other rule of thumb: *Volume generally precedes price.* A professional trader will notice a decline in volume before an uptrend starts to run out of steam.

In Figure 6.1, we see confirmation—from December through February volume increases as prices move up.

In Figure 6.2, with decreasing volume from the middle of November through early January, we can assume that corn's uptrend will slow or flatten, which it did. This is an example of divergence.

FIGURE 6.1 Example of Increasing Volume

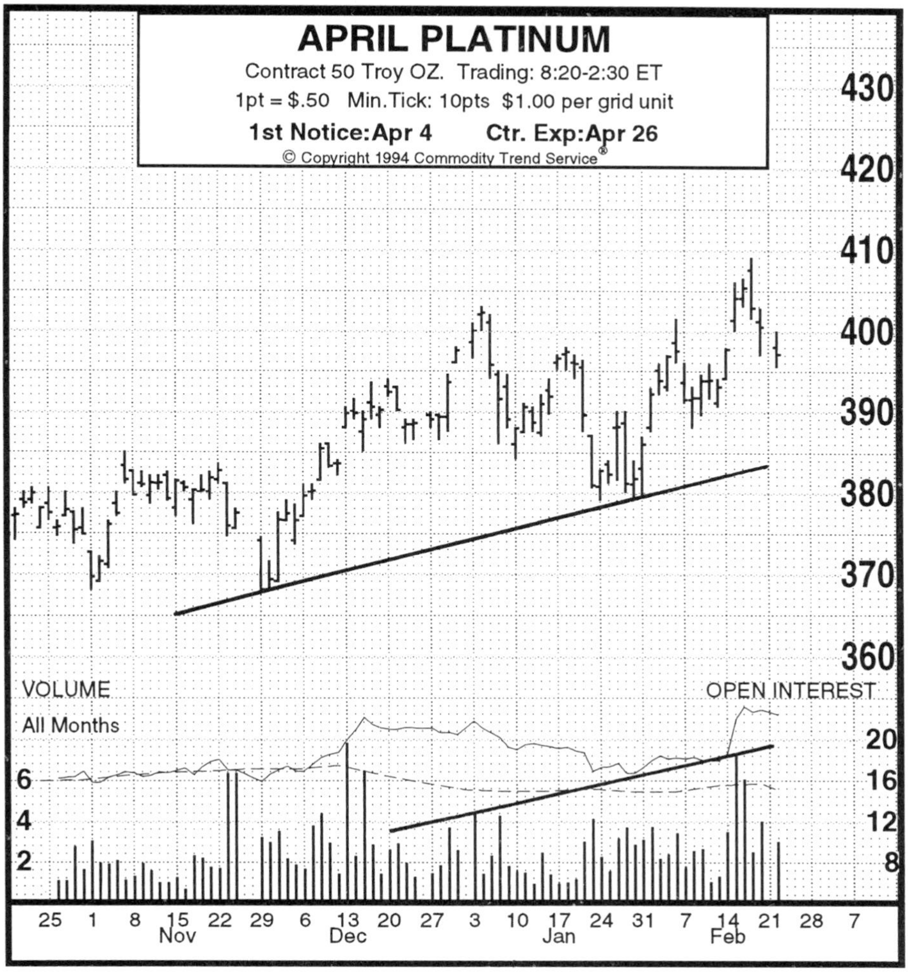
APRIL PLATINUM
Contract 50 Troy OZ. Trading: 8:20-2:30 ET
1pt = $.50 Min.Tick: 10pts $1.00 per grid unit
1st Notice:Apr 4 Ctr. Exp:Apr 26
© Copyright 1994 Commodity Trend Service®
430
420
410
400
390
380
370
360
VOLUME
All Months
OPEN INTEREST
6
4
2
20
16
12
8
25 1 8 15 22 29 6 13 20 27 3 10 17 24 31 7 14 21 28 7
Nov
Dec
Jan
Feb

FIGURE 6.2 Example of Decreasing Volume

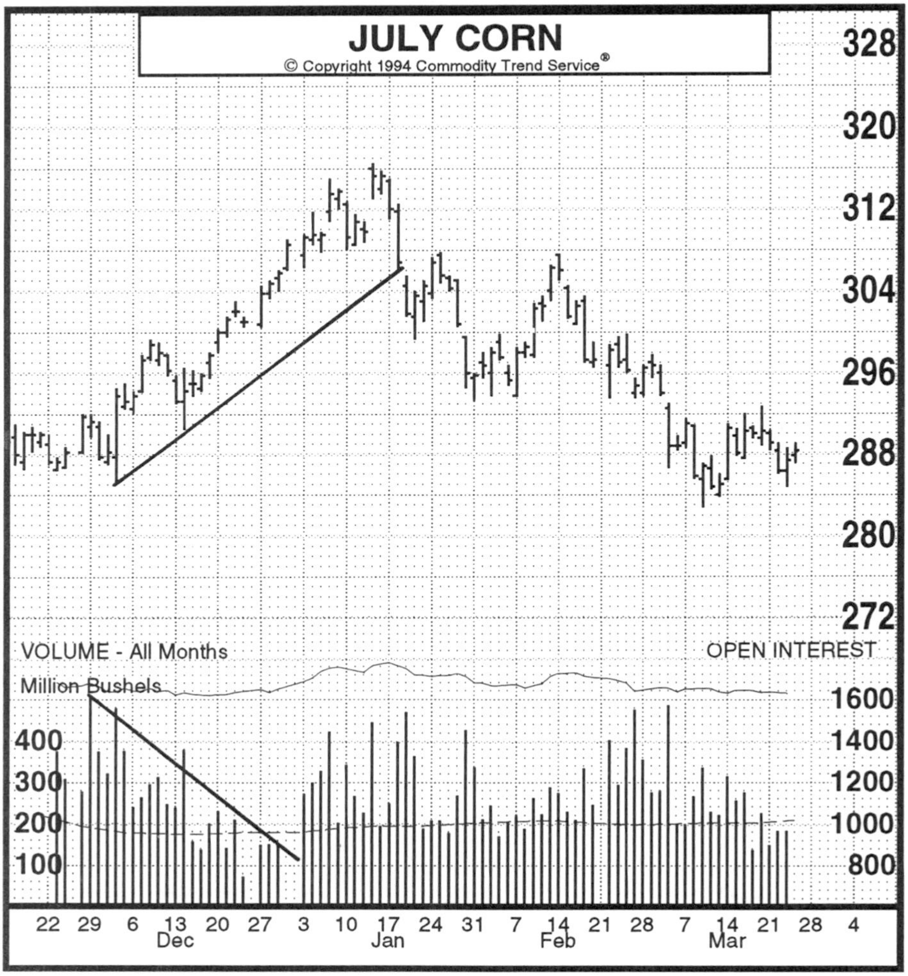
JULY CORN
© Copyright 1994 Commodity Trend Service®
328
320
312
304
296
288
280
272
VOLUME - All Months
Million Bushels
OPEN INTEREST
1600
1400
1200
1000
800
400
300
200
100
22 29 6 13 20 27 3 10 17 24 31 7 14 21 28 7 14 21 28 4
Dec
Jan
Feb
Mar

OPEN INTEREST

Open interest is the total number of outstanding contracts held at the end of the day. It is the total of all longs or shorts, but not both, since there has to be a long and a short for every contract—and there is no need to count them twice.

Open interest is drawn as a solid line along the bottom of the chart, near the volume.

Open interest sometimes confuses people, but it is really very easy to understand. Here is a simple example:

Day #1   Two people went long and bought a contract each and two other people went short and sold a contract each.
Result: Volume: 2   Open interest: 2

Day #2   The next day, three contracts were bought and three contracts were sold.
Result: Volume: 3   Open interest: 5 (There are five contracts outstanding.)

Day #3   One of our existing contract holders decided to offset his position and sell back his long position.
Result: Volume: 1   Open interest: 4

Early in a futures contract's life, open interest is small, but it builds as the contract reaches maturity. Naturally, as the contract approaches expiration, open interest declines as traders liquidate their open positions.

Open interest is very similar to volume; that is, if prices are moving up and open interest is also increasing, that is a confirming signal. It means that more new buyers are coming in.

When open interest starts to decline during an uptrend, your uptrend may have run its course. You may find that prices continue to move up for a while. That could be because shorts may be getting out and prices are advancing primarily on short covering—not new buying.

The same holds true in a downtrend. You want to see open interest increasing. In Figure 6.3, you see confirmation—increasing open interest as the downtrend continues.

FIGURE 6.3   Example of Increasing Open Interest

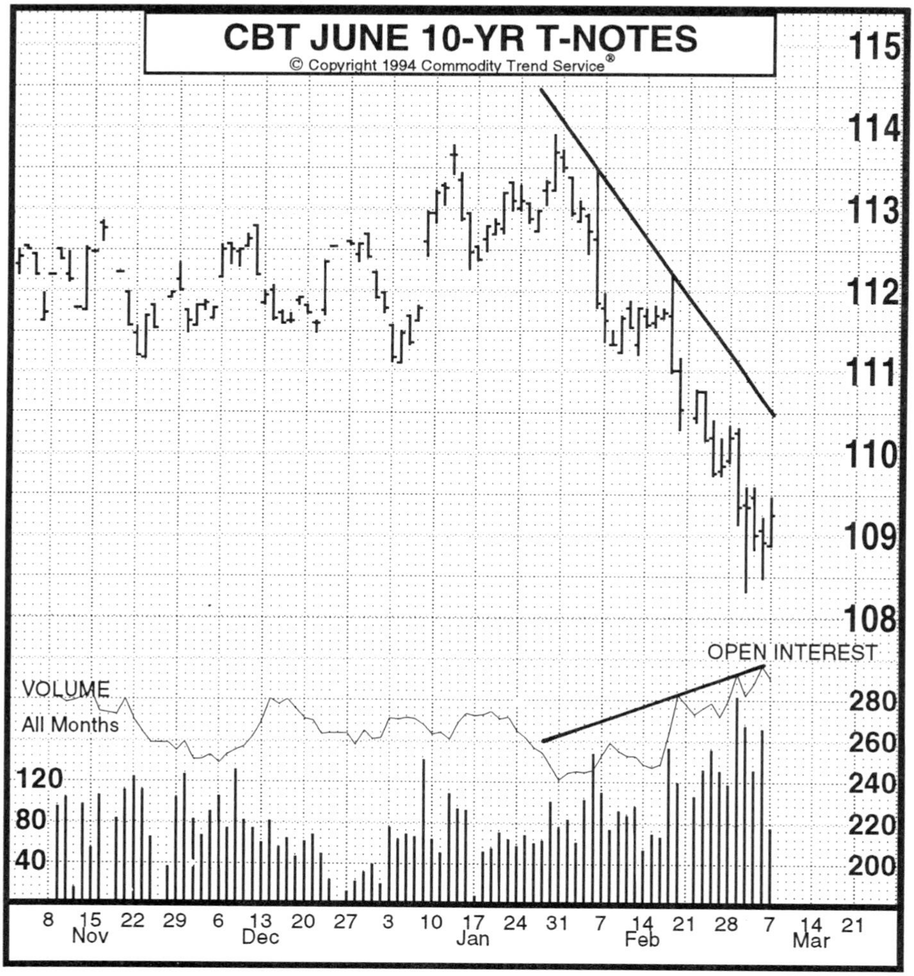

In Figure 6.4, we see open interest decreasing for the period January through the middle of March as prices also decrease. This indicates that the downward trend may have run its course and the uptrend could resume.

FIGURE 6.4   Example of Decreasing Open Interest

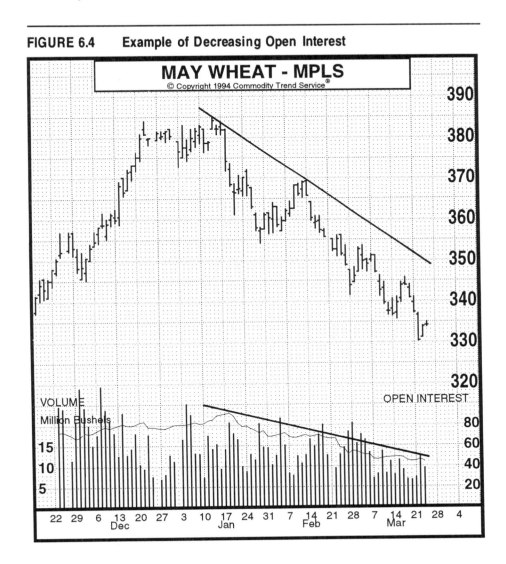

Figures 6.5 and 6.7 give you the opportunity to work on two examples.
Figures 6.6 and 6.8 show the answers. Look at volume and open interest.
Draw lines that show increasing or decreasing activity and see how they
relate to prices. Where you see confirmation, note that area of the chart and
mark it "confirmation." If there is divergence, mark it "divergence."

FIGURE 6.5   YOU CAN DO IT
Analyze Volume and Open Interest
Number 1

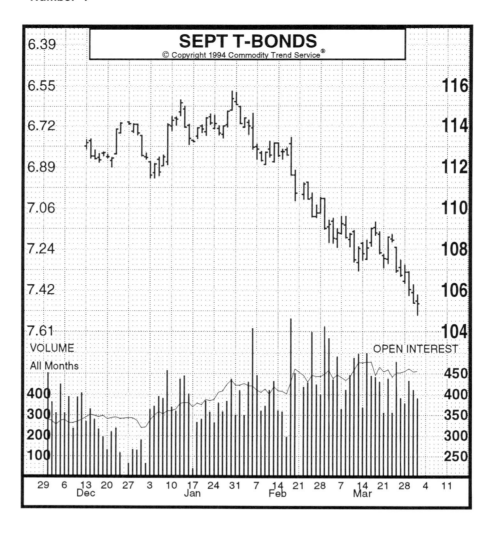

FIGURE 6.6   **ANSWER**
Volume and Open Interest
Number 1

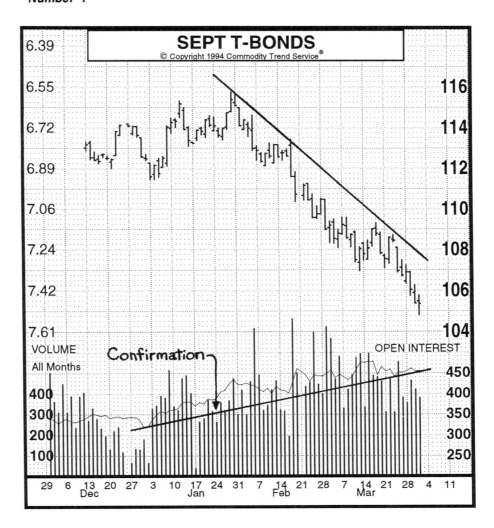

FIGURE 6.7   YOU CAN DO IT
Analyze Volume and Open Interest
Number 2

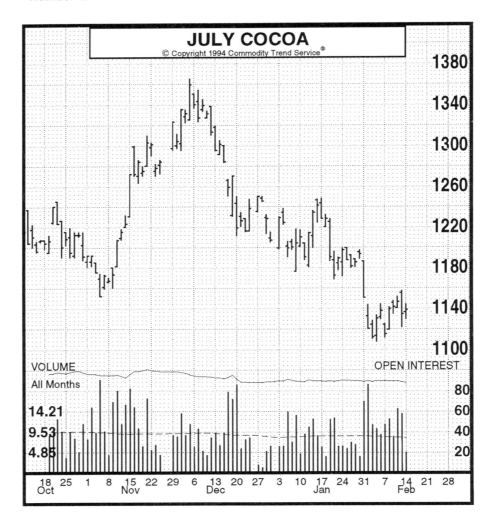

FIGURE 6.8 **ANSWER**
Volume and Open Interest
Number 2

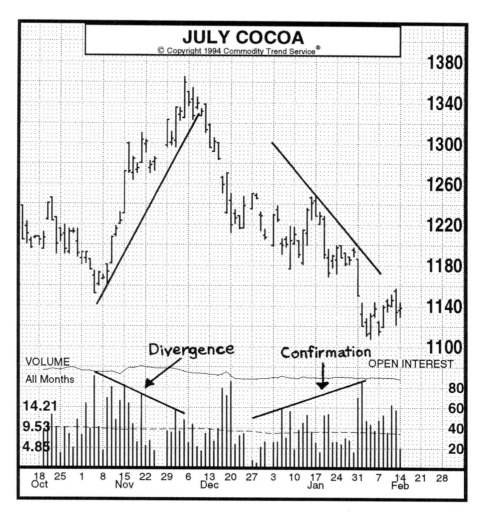

7 | GOING WITH THE FLOW—CONTINUATION PATTERNS

You could trade the futures markets on just price, volume and open interest. But that is not the way the professionals do it. They realize that prices rarely move in straight lines. They look for patterns to help them find a clear-cut entry or exit point.

This chapter, and Chapters 8 and 9, will help you identify patterns. This chapter examines continuation patterns; Chapter 8 examines gaps, and Chapter 9 goes in the opposite direction with reversal patterns.

CONTINUATION PATTERNS

Continuation patterns are usually sideways price formations that represent a pause in a major trend. After the pause (which could run days or even a few weeks) the major trend continues.

Flags

One class of continuation patterns are *flags*. Flags are small parallelograms that often form right after a rapid price move. They are among the most reliable continuation patterns.

Flags can be either *bull flags* or *bear flags*. A bull flag is found in an uptrend, while a bear flag is located in a downtrend.

At first, you may find these flags a little confusing. That is because a bull flag slopes downward, while a bear flag moves up. The designation of the flag refers to the major trend that it is in. Hence, a bull flag is in a rising market. Flags illustrate profit-taking by short-term traders.

Flags generally run for a few days. Volume tends to decrease when a flag is forming, reflecting a pattern of hiatus in a recently active market.

What purpose do they serve? An excellent rule of thumb often used by chartists is that a flag marks the approximate halfway point of a price move. Flags can give you a good indication of how much further a trend line will continue.

Notice that the bull flag shown in Figure 7.1 is approximately halfway along the trend line, as most flags are. Even though the parallelogram is pointing down, it is considered a bull flag because the overall trend line is upward. As flags generally appear halfway along a trend line, one can make a reasonable target price by adding the first leg to the breakout point on the flag. Figure 7.2 is an example of a bear flag.

Pennants

Pennants are similar to flags, except that they are small triangular formations rather than parallelograms. Because flags and pennants are easily identifiable and develop only after a clear short-term or intermediate-term trend has been established, they can be an especially valuable charting tool.

To determine a reasonable target price, measure the widest part of the pennant and add that distance to the price at the breakout point. In Figure 7.3, the widest distance was 5.40 (89.40 minus 84.00), which is added to the breakout price of 87.40 for a target price of 92.80.

FIGURE 7.1   Example of a Bull Flag

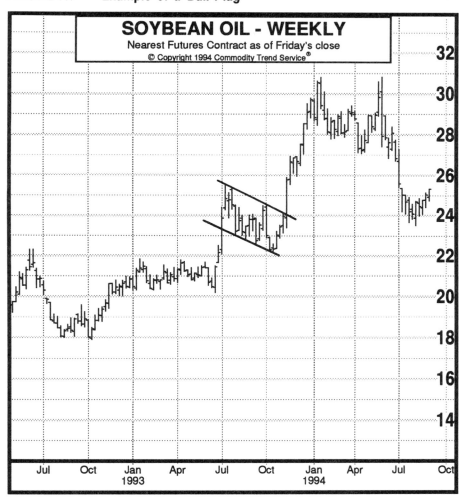

FIGURE 7.2   Example of a Bear Flag

SEPTEMBER EURODOLLAR

© Copyright 1994 Commodity Trend Service®

FIGURE 7.3   Example of a Pennant

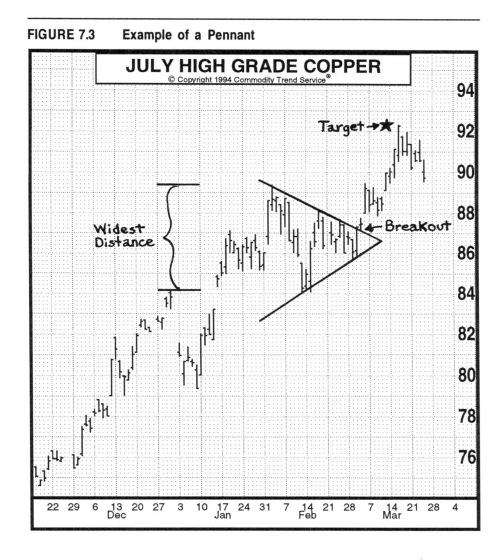

YOU
CAN
DO IT

In Figures 7.4–7.15, you will have several chances to chart flags and pennants. After you have drawn your parallelogram or triangle, mark "target" where you think the target price of the major trend will continue to move.

FIGURE 7.4 **YOU CAN DO IT**
Chart a Bull Flag
Number 1

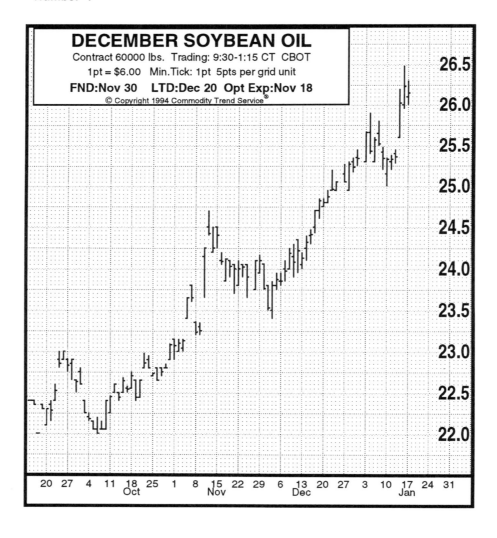

DECEMBER SOYBEAN OIL
Contract 60000 lbs. Trading: 9:30-1:15 CT CBOT
1pt = $6.00   Min.Tick: 1pt 5pts per grid unit
FND:Nov 30   LTD:Dec 20 Opt Exp:Nov 18
© Copyright 1994 Commodity Trend Service®

FIGURE 7.5 **ANSWER**
Bull Flag
Number 1

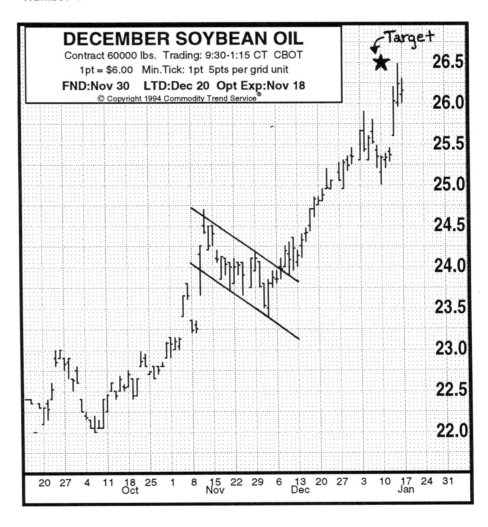

FIGURE 7.6   YOU CAN DO IT
Chart a Bull Flag
Number 2

FIGURE 7.7   ANSWER
Bull Flag
Number 2

FIGURE 7.8   **YOU CAN DO IT**
Chart a Bear Flag
Number 1

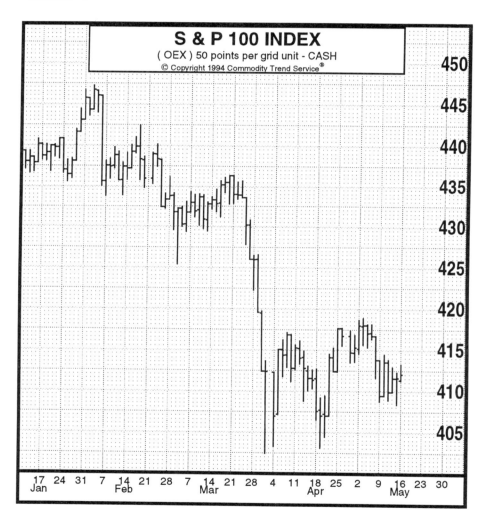

FIGURE 7.9   **ANSWER**
Bear Flag
Number 1

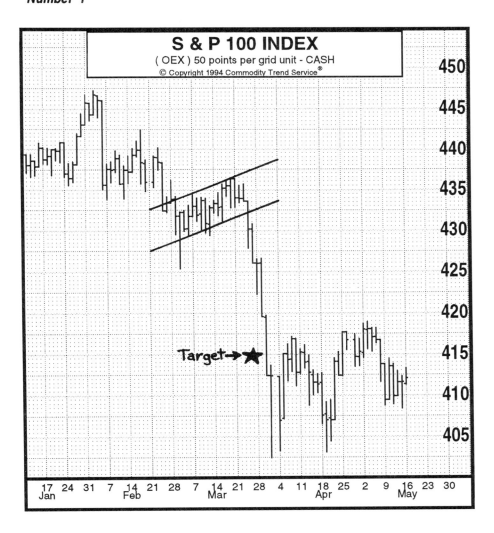

FIGURE 7.10   **YOU CAN DO IT**
Chart a Bear Flag
Number 2

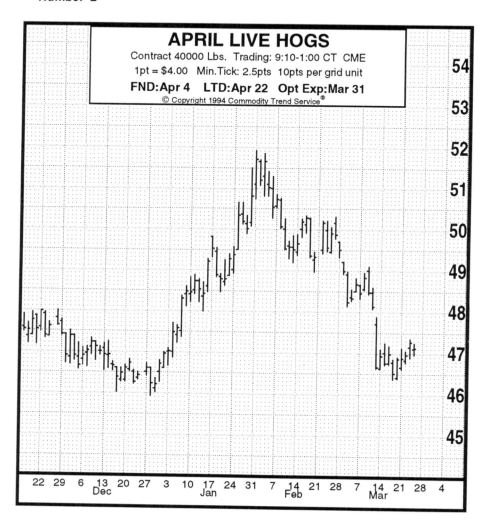

FIGURE 7.11   **ANSWER**
Bear Flag
Number 2

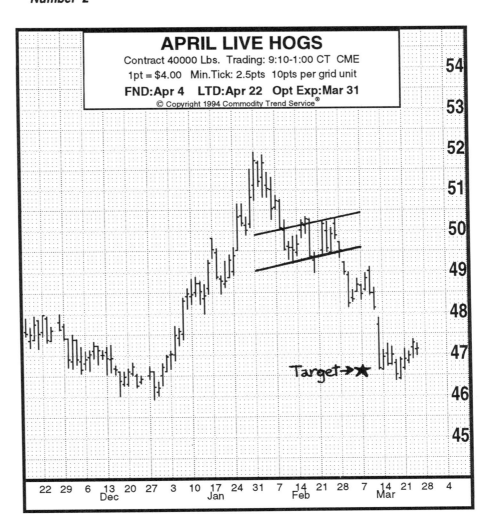

APRIL LIVE HOGS

Contract 40000 Lbs. Trading: 9:10-1:00 CT CME

1pt = $4.00   Min.Tick: 2.5pts 10pts per grid unit

FND:Apr 4   LTD:Apr 22   Opt Exp:Mar 31

© Copyright 1994 Commodity Trend Service®

Target→★

FIGURE 7.12   **YOU CAN DO IT**
Chart a Pennant
Number 1

FIGURE 7.13   **ANSWER**
Pennant
Number 1

FIGURE 7.14   **YOU CAN DO IT**
Chart a Pennant
Number 2

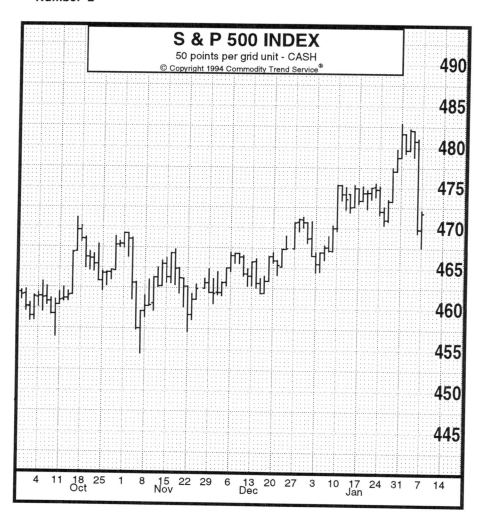

FIGURE 7.15   **ANSWER**
Pennant
Number 2

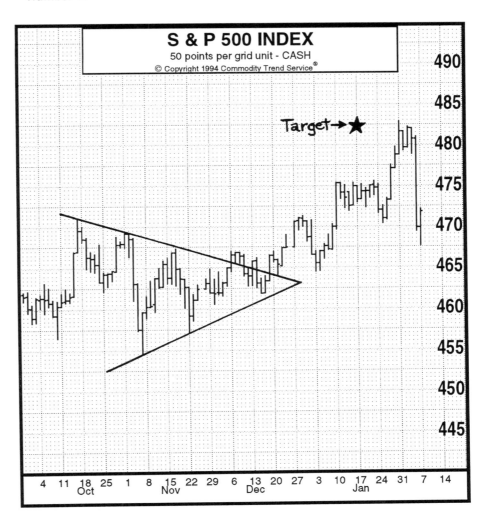

Triangles

Triangles form when short-term uptrend and downtrend lines intersect. Their meaning is similar to those of flags and pennants, but triangles may take several weeks to form on daily charts. There are three types of triangles— ascending, descending and symmetrical.

An *ascending triangle* is considered bullish. The upper trend line is a resistance area. The lower line has an upward slope. As buyers become more aggressive, there is a breakout—that is why ascending triangles are bullish.

To estimate a target price, measure the widest distance of the triangle and add it to the breakout price. In Figure 7.16, the widest distance is 85, which is added to the breakout price of 1775, for a target of 1860.

Remember that patterns do not help you as an investor unless you can utilize the information. When faced with an ascending triangle, measure the widest point of the triangle. You can use that distance as a potential target for the breakout. Now you have a reasonable objective for an intermediate price move.

Descending triangles have the same components as ascending triangles, except that they break through a support area as opposed to a resistance area. When the selling pressure exceeds the buying support, the trend continues downward. In Figure 7.17, we see a two-year descending triangle with a target price of 12.

Symmetrical triangles are very similar in appearance to pennants; however, they run longer in duration. With a symmetrical triangle, a large move can go in either an up or down direction. More often than not, the breakout will occur in the same direction as the original trend.

FIGURE 7.16   Example of an Ascending Triangle

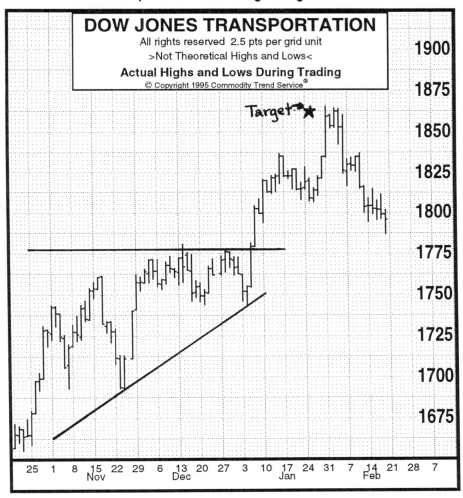

DOW JONES TRANSPORTATION

Target★

FIGURE 7.17   Example of a Descending Triangle

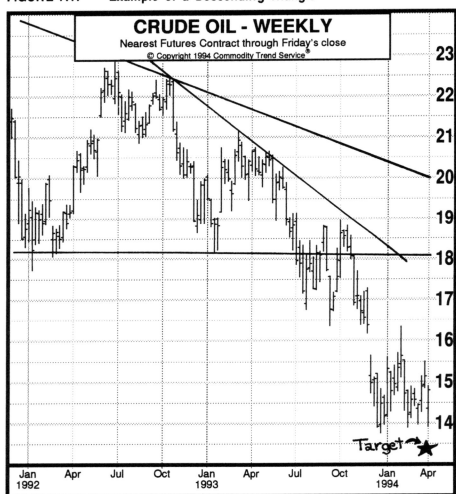

CRUDE OIL - WEEKLY

Nearest Futures Contract through Friday's close

© Copyright 1994 Commodity Trend Service®

YOU CAN DO IT

Figures 7.18–7.29 mark not only the triangle, but the support or resistance areas as well, and indicate your anticipated target price. In the example shown in Figure 7.21, the target was reached and exceeded. Note how the support line was prematurely violated; the pattern, however, maintained its overall shape.

FIGURE 7.18   **YOU CAN DO IT**
Chart an Ascending Triangle
Number 1

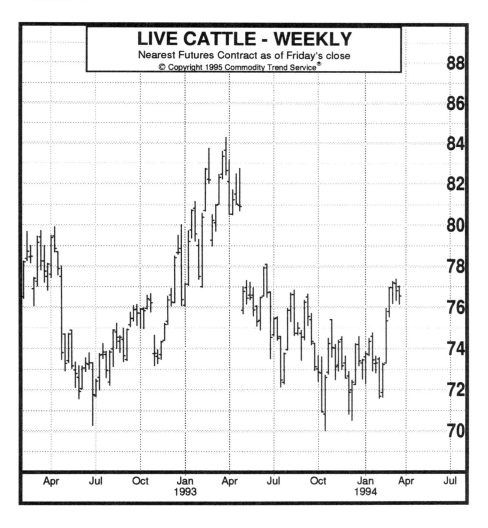

FIGURE 7.19   **ANSWER**
Ascending Triangle
Number 1

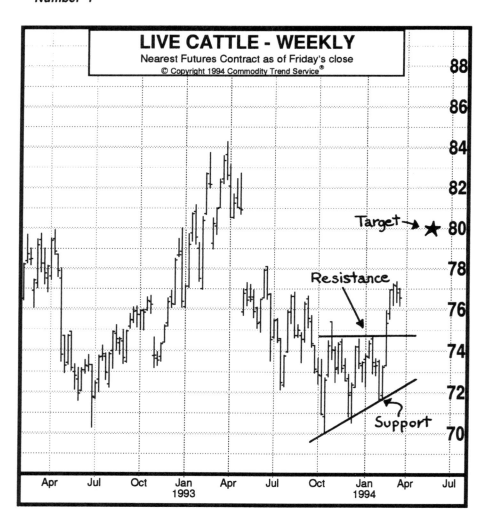

FIGURE 7.20   **YOU CAN DO IT**
Chart an Ascending Triangle
Number 2

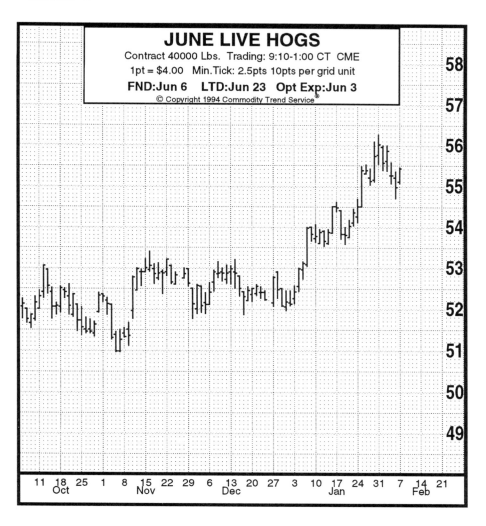

In the example shown in Figure 7.21, the target was reached and exceeded.

FIGURE 7.21   ANSWER
Ascending Triangle
Number 2

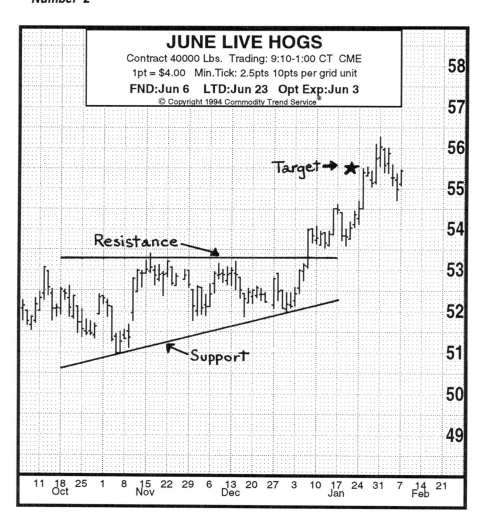

FIGURE 7.22   YOU CAN DO IT
Chart a Descending Triangle
Number 1

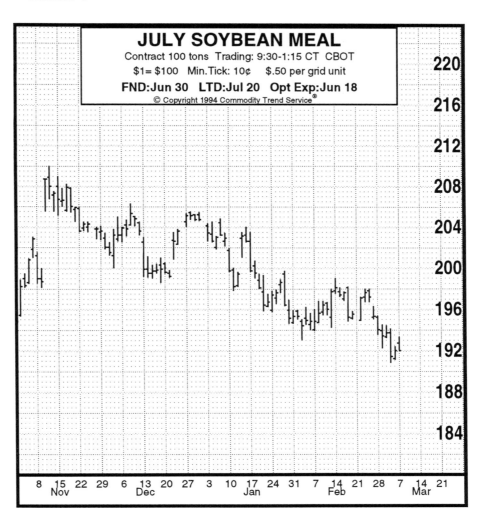

JULY SOYBEAN MEAL
Contract 100 tons Trading: 9:30-1:15 CT CBOT
$1= $100   Min.Tick: 10¢ $.50 per grid unit
FND:Jun 30   LTD:Jul 20   Opt Exp:Jun 18
© Copyright 1994 Commodity Trend Service®

Note how the support line was prematurely violated; the pattern, however, maintained its overall shape.

FIGURE 7.23   **ANSWER**
Descending Triangle
Number 1

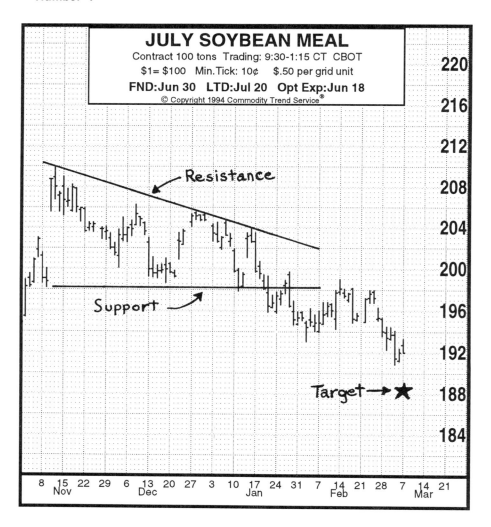

FIGURE 7.24 **YOU CAN DO IT**
Chart a Descending Triangle
Number 2

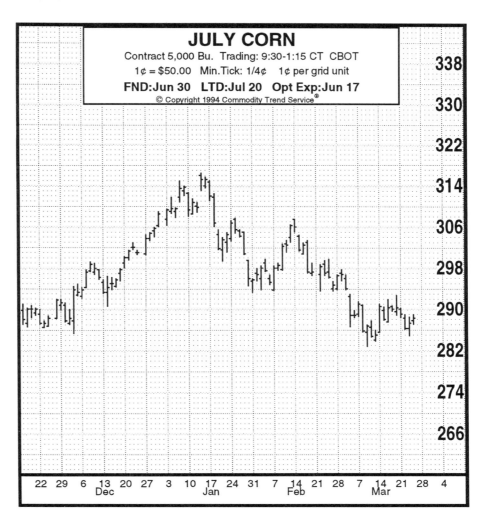

JULY CORN
Contract 5,000 Bu. Trading: 9:30-1:15 CT CBOT
1¢ = $50.00 Min.Tick: 1/4¢ 1¢ per grid unit
FND:Jun 30 LTD:Jul 20 Opt Exp:Jun 17
© Copyright 1994 Commodity Trend Service®

FIGURE 7.25   **ANSWER**
Descending Triangle
Number 2

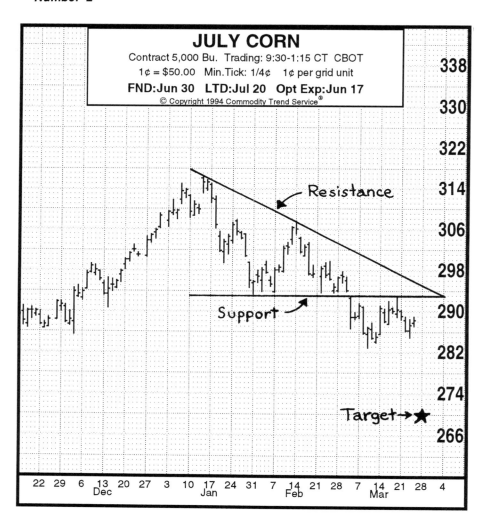

FIGURE 7.26   YOU CAN DO IT
Chart a Symmetrical Triangle
Number 1

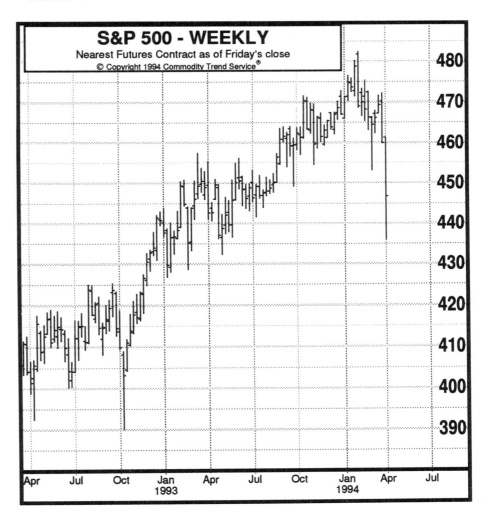

FIGURE 7.27   **ANSWER**
                    Symmetrical Triangle
                    Number 1

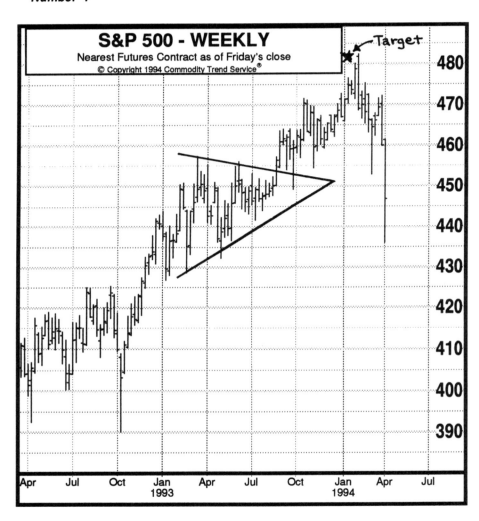

FIGURE 7.28   **YOU CAN DO IT**
Chart a Symmetrical Triangle
Number 2

FIGURE 7.29   **ANSWER**
Symmetrical Triangle
Number 2

COFFEE - WEEKLY
Nearest Futures Contract as of Friday's close
© Copyright 1995 Commodity Trend Service®

8

WHERE NO ACTIVITY
SAYS A LOT—GAPS

The dictionary defines a gap as a break, an opening or an interval. In terms of spotting profitable patterns, an empty space can say a lot about a trend's direction.

Gaps are easy to spot and analyze. But just because they are easy to pinpoint, don't think they are not valuable. Professional traders understand the importance of gaps and how to use them in their analysis. Knowing how to use gaps can give you an edge in profitable futures trading.

GAPS

Gaps are simply price ranges on a chart where no actual trading has taken place. They form when prices open higher or lower than the previous day's range. All gaps are not the same. To become a knowledgeable trader, you must be able to distinguish four different types of gaps.

Common Gaps

The *common gap* is the least important of all gaps because it is assumed to have no special meaning or prognostication capability. It can occur in thinly traded markets, or it can be found in the midst of a sideways channel. Prices return to fill common gaps, usually within a few days.

Breakaway Gaps

A *breakaway gap* often occurs at the end of a sideways consolidation pattern. It signals the beginning of a significant price move, which may be very dynamic.

Breakaway gaps are normally not filled for several weeks or months. As a rule of thumb, the greater the volume at a breakaway gap, the less likely prices will retract and fill.

Breakaway gaps that occur at the upper end of the channel are referred to as upside gaps. When the market corrects and comes down in price, these gaps can act as support areas. Conversely, downside gaps (found at the lower level of a channel) can act as resistance areas when prices move up after a downward move.

Measuring Gaps

Measuring gaps or *runaway gaps* occur after a trend is already established. They are significant because they generally mark the midpoint of a move. You might say that the market is moving effortlessly, and that is reason for the jumps in price.

Measuring gaps can also act as support and resistance areas when price corrections occur in a major trend.

Exhaustion Gaps

As the name suggests, an *exhaustion gap* occurs during the final stages of a move. It usually occurs within a couple days of a climax top or bottom.

An exhaustion gap reflects a market that simply runs out of steam. When prices close under this last gap, it usually foreshadows the start of a sideways pattern or a reversal of the prior major trend.

In Figures 8.1 and 8.2, a variety of different gaps are shown in the same chart.

FIGURE 8.1   **Examples of Gaps**
                  Number 1

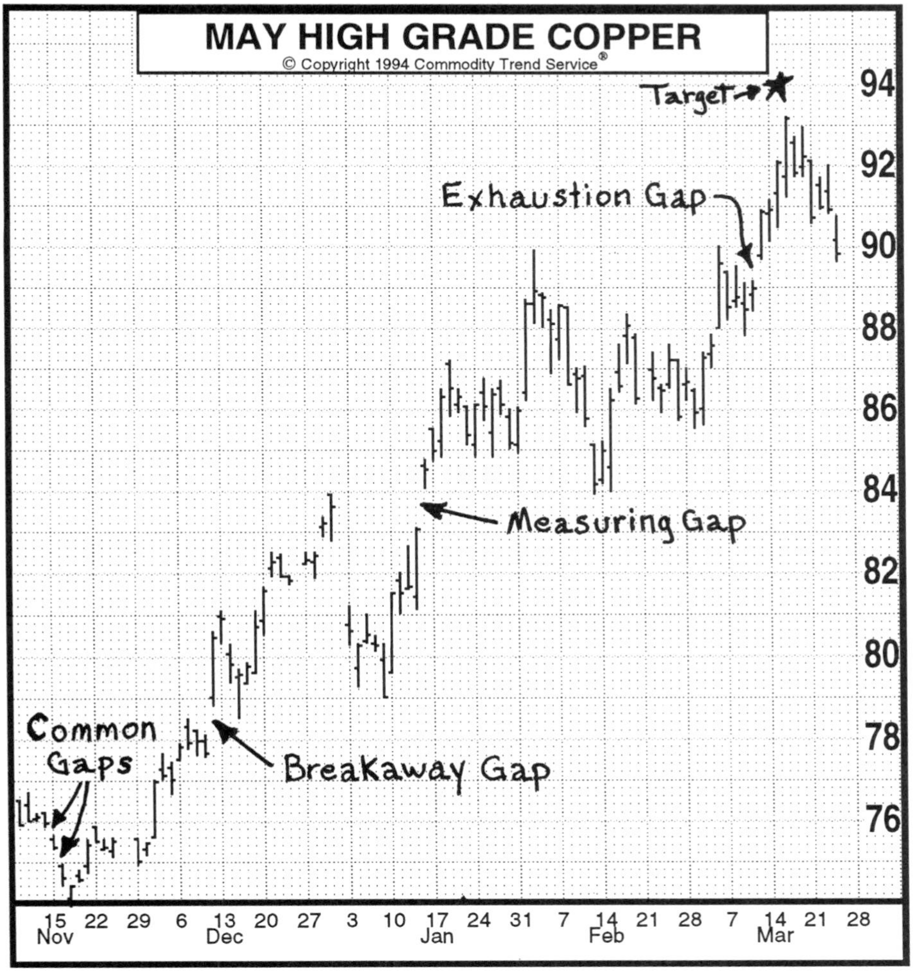

MAY HIGH GRADE COPPER
© Copyright 1994 Commodity Trend Service®

FIGURE 8.2   Examples of Gaps
Number 2

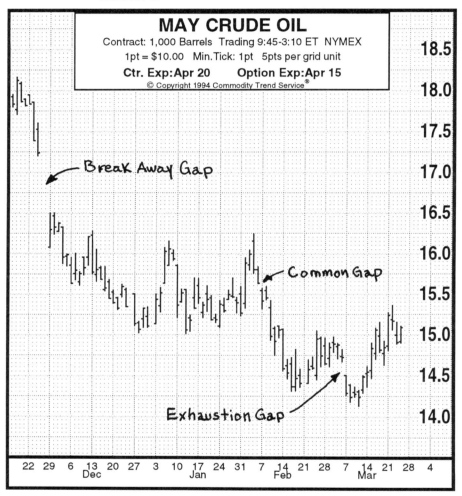

YOU
CAN
DO IT

In Figures 8.3–8.6, find gaps located in each chart and label them. In the case of measuring gaps, mark a target price you think is a reasonable objective.

FIGURE 8.3   YOU CAN DO IT
Indicate the Gaps
Number 1

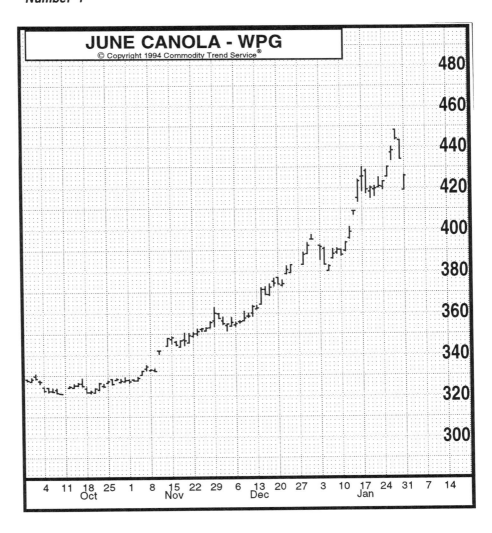

FIGURE 8.4   **ANSWER**
Gaps
Number 1

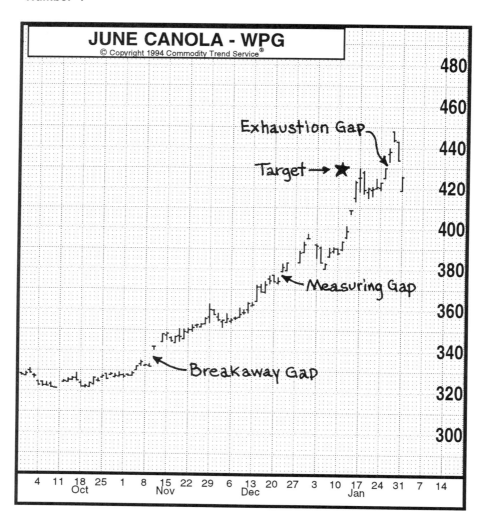

FIGURE 8.5 **YOU CAN DO IT**
Indicate the Gaps
Number 2

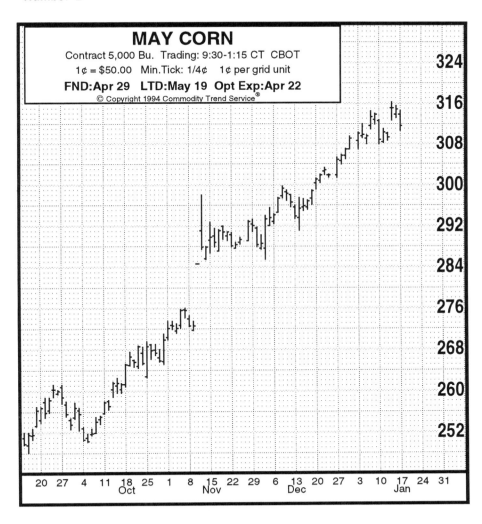

MAY CORN
Contract 5,000 Bu. Trading: 9:30-1:15 CT CBOT
1¢ = $50.00   Min.Tick: 1/4¢   1¢ per grid unit
FND:Apr 29   LTD:May 19 Opt Exp:Apr 22
© Copyright 1994 Commodity Trend Service®

FIGURE 8.6   ANSWER
Gaps
Number 2

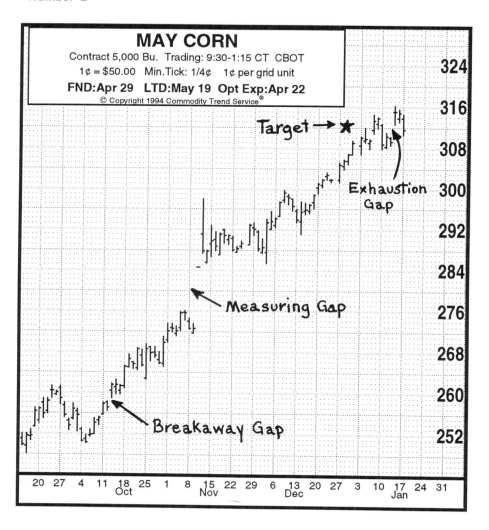

9 | CHANGING DIRECTION— REVERSAL PATTERNS

By now, the reason for grouping Chapters 7, 8 and 9 should be clear. Because successful traders go long or short in the direction of the major trend, the continuation patterns you learned in Chapter 7 helped to define the direction of the primary trend. Chapter 8 closed with the exhaustion gap—which could very well indicate the top (or bottom) of a primary trend.

In futures trading, what goes up must come down (and vice versa), so you need to be alert to reversal patterns. For example, if you were long futures contracts, reversal patterns can help you take your profits and assume new short positions. Remember, professional traders don't care which way the market is traveling, as long as they are trading in the right direction.

REVERSAL PATTERNS

As the name suggests, *reversal patterns* are formations that indicate a trend is about to make a significant change in direction.

Keep in mind that a reversal pattern exists only if there is a prior opposite trend against which to compare it. So don't bother looking for patterns without that prior trend.

It would be nice if all reversal patterns were quickly and easily defined, but actually most trend changes happen over a period of time. Be careful: A trend may look as if it is reversing when it is consolidating instead. If you are new to the field, it might be better to wait a few days to see if the reversal takes hold. While you may miss the absolute top or bottom of a market, you can still generate plenty of profits once you know a new trend line has been established.

Although most reversal patterns do take time to emerge, one is very quick—a reversal day pattern.

Reversal Day

While some technicians would not necessarily call a single *reversal day* a pattern, it is one formation that signals a top or a bottom of a trend. There can be top reversal days and bottom reversal days, which usually occur after a sizable rally.

What happens on a typical top reversal day? See Figure 9.1 for an example. Usually, a run-up of prices occurs early in the day, reaching a new high. By the end of the day, however, prices have retreated and the closing price is lower than the previous day. Reversal tops are often followed by abrupt collapses.

How do you know if you really have a reversal day on your charts? You have to look at two factors: the distance of the range and the volume. If you have a range that covers a wide price move and volume is heavy, you can expect a reversal.

Island Reversal

When a cluster of days stands apart from the rest of the prices around them, you have an *island reversal* pattern. Take a look at the island reversal top pattern in Figure 9.2. It almost looks like an island above a body of water.

An island reversal is surrounded by two gaps. On the left is an exhaustion gap, because of the rapid run of prices. On the right is a breakaway gap, because of the minichannel that preceded it.

FIGURE 9.1   Example of a Reversal Day

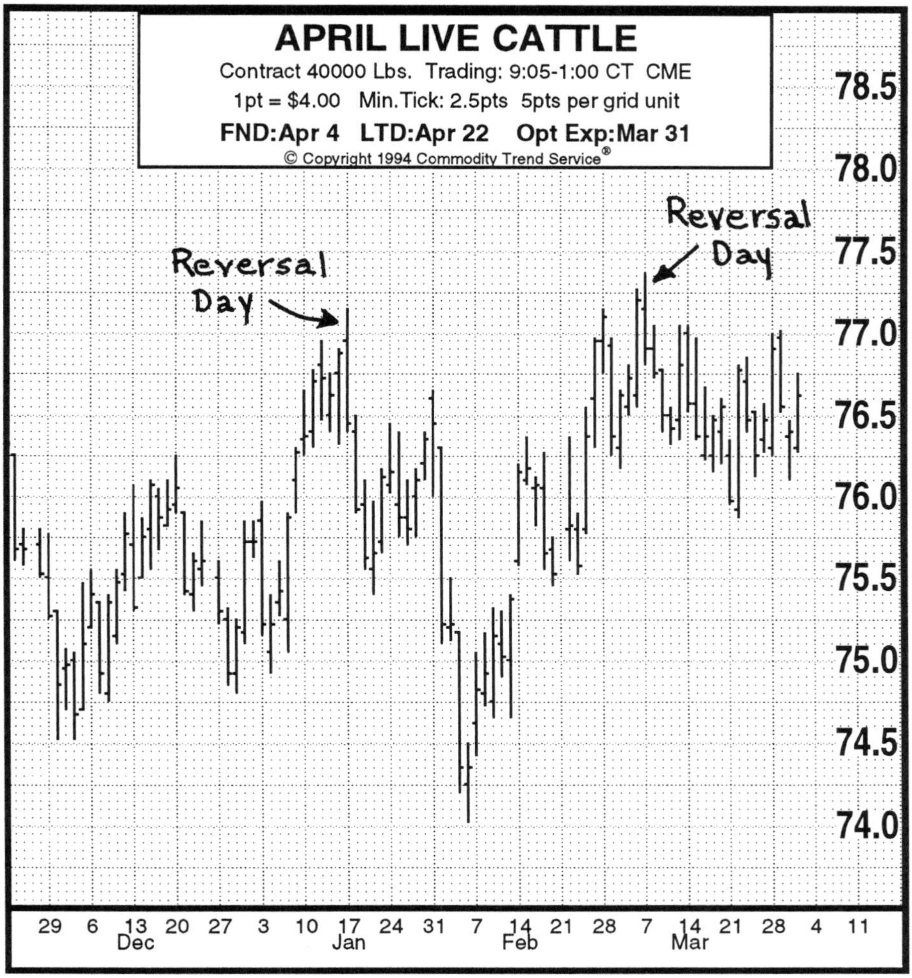

FIGURE 9.2   Example of an Island Reversal

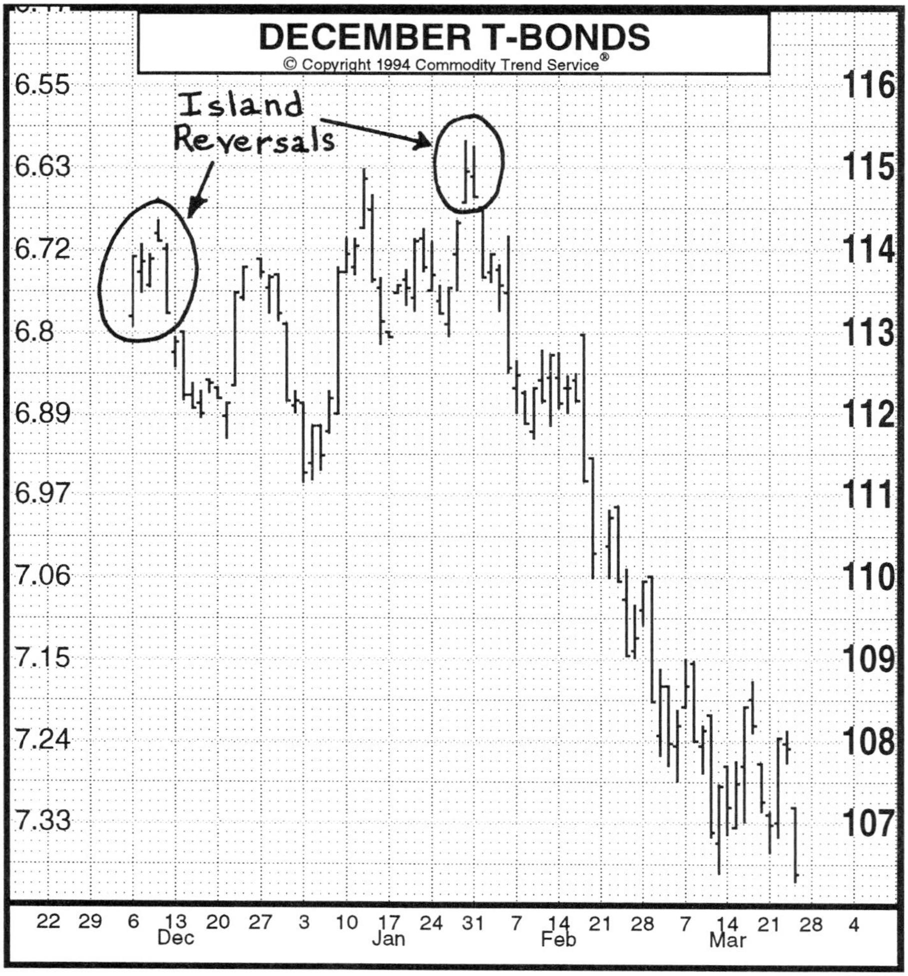

Head and Shoulders

A *head-and-shoulders* pattern is one of the best known and most reliable of reversal patterns. It consists of two shoulders and a head. It can exist at a market top or bottom. Notice in Figure 9.3 that the neckline is drawn across the bottom of both shoulders. By using the vertical distance from the head to the neckline, you can project a target price.

FIGURE 9.3   Example of a Head-and-Shoulders Pattern

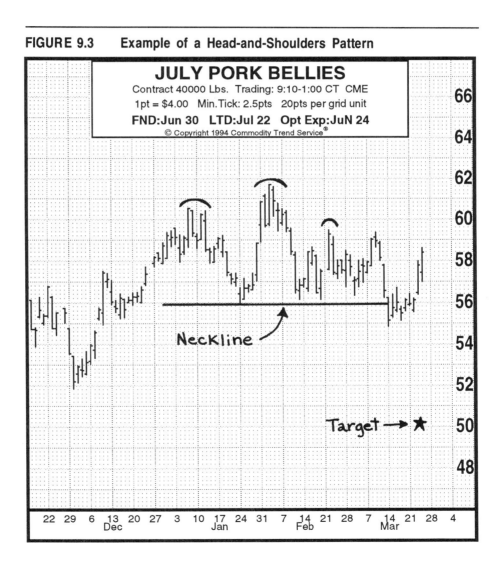

At a market top, the head is the highest part of the formation. At a market bottom, the head is the lowest part.

In a textbook-perfect formation, both shoulders are about the same height. Volume is heavy on the left shoulder, but lighter during the head and right shoulder.

A top head-and-shoulders formation is considered complete when a neckline is drawn across the bottom of both shoulders, as in Figure 9.3. In a bottom head and shoulder, the neckline is drawn across the top of the upside-down shoulders.

A head-and-shoulder formation can help you in two ways:

1. It can indicate that a trend has made a major reversal. If you were long a position before, it is time to consider going short.
2. It also can help by giving you some price projections. Measure the vertical distance from the top of the head to the neckline. Use this distance as a projection for a price target.

Because head-and-shoulder formations serve two functions, professional traders rely heavily on these formations when they come across them.

Double Tops and Bottoms

A *double top* is formed by a peak, a valley, a second peak that stops at about the same level of the first peak and finally a drop in prices that falls below the previous valley. Some chartists call this an *M*.

A *double bottom* is the inverse of a top, forming a *W*.

Double tops and bottoms are more common than head and shoulders, but they are not as reliable—perhaps because this pattern is two tries for a trend line change instead of three tries. An example of a double top is shown in Figure 9.4.

FIGURE 9.4   Example of a Double Top

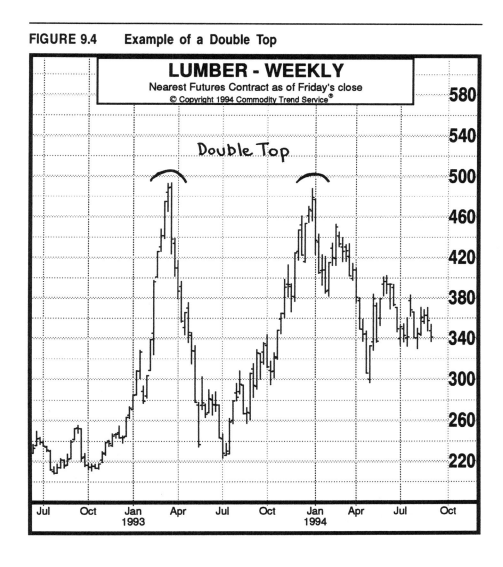

YOU
CAN
DO IT

Figures 9.5–9.10 give you some practice identifying reversal patterns. Try to find and label as many as you can.

FIGURE 9.5   **YOU CAN DO IT**
Identify Reversal Patterns
Number 1

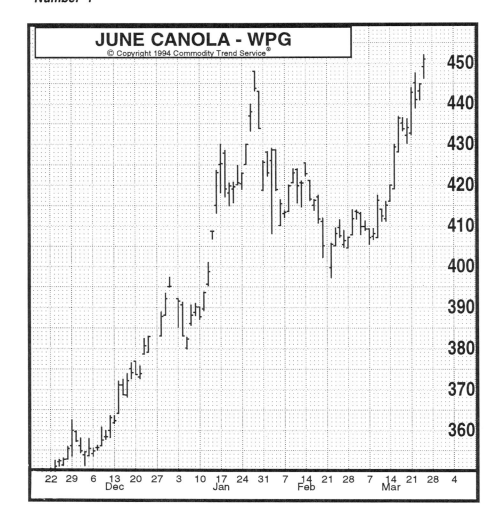

FIGURE 9.6   **ANSWER**
Reversal Patterns
Number 1

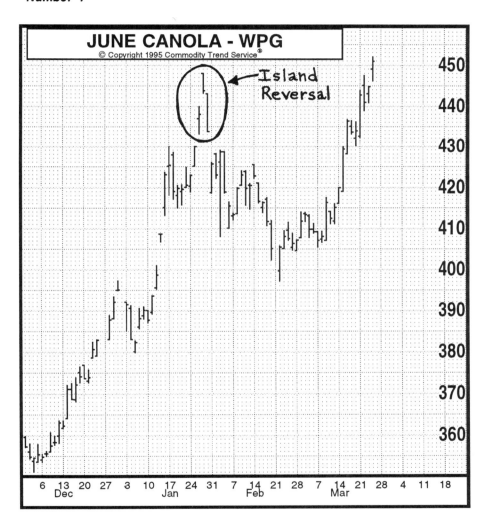

JUNE CANOLA - WPG
© Copyright 1995 Commodity Trend Service®

Island Reversal

FIGURE 9.7   YOU CAN DO IT
Identify Reversal Patterns
Number 2

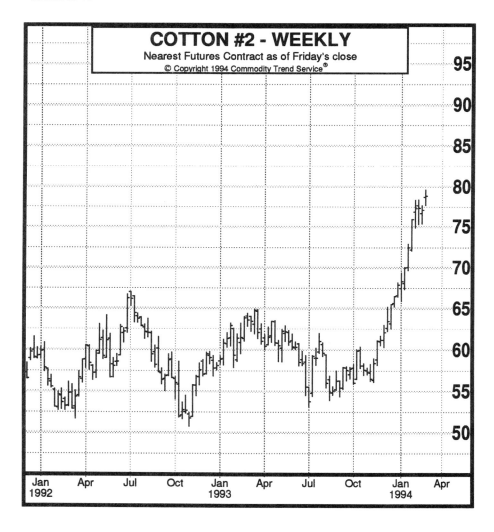

FIGURE 9.8   **ANSWER**
Reversal Patterns
Number 2

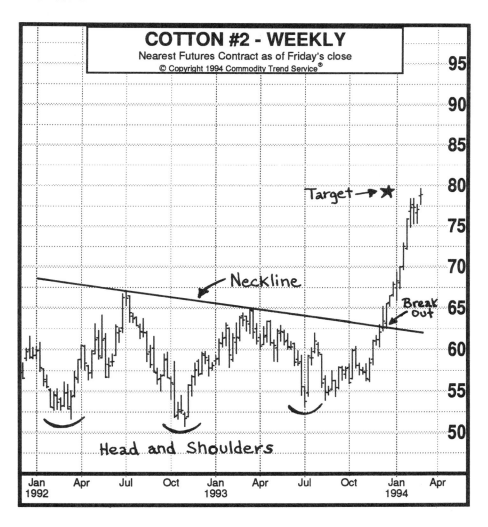

FIGURE 9.9   **YOU CAN DO IT**
Identify Reversal Patterns
Number 3

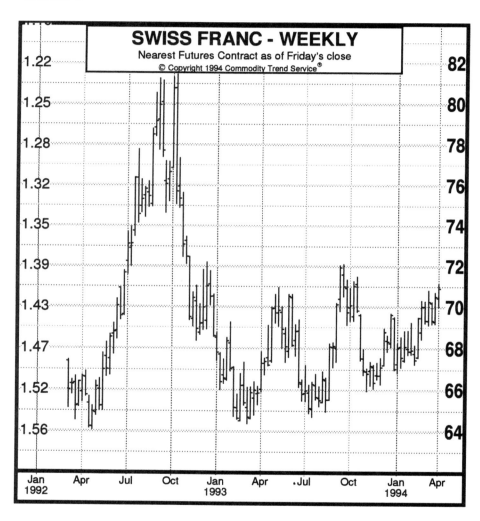

FIGURE 9.10   **ANSWER**
Reversal Patterns
Number 3

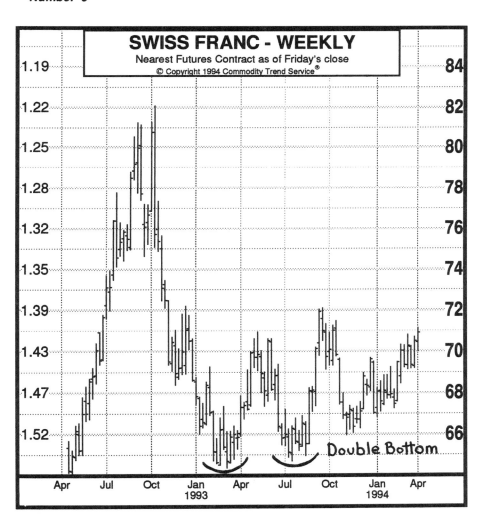

10 | A Tried and Proven Tool— Moving Averages

While two chartists may disagree on whether a particular pattern is a symmetrical triangle or a pennant, both can understand and appreciate the power of moving averages. It is not surprising that it is one of the most widely used tools among full-time futures traders.

MOVING AVERAGES

An *average* is the intermediate value of a series of numbers. For a nine-day average, you would take the closing prices of a futures contract for the past nine days, compute the sum and divide by nine.

But the market changes daily. To create an ongoing nine-day moving average, every day we would drop the ninth day back and add today's new closing prices.

A *moving average* is a trend-following device. It helps you see when an old trend has reversed and a new trend has begun. It does not have any predictive qualities. It can, however, provide excellent guidance.

Traders constantly look at rapidly changing developments that occur in a market. But if you're too close to the trees, you cannot easily see the forest. By their very nature, moving averages smooth out a pricing pattern, making it much easier to see an underlying trend.

You could use any number of moving averages. A 4-day, 9-day, 18-day and 40-day moving average can provide a wealth of information. Figures 10.1 and 10.2 show sample moving average charts.

FIGURE 10.1   Example of a 4-Day, 9-Day and 18-Day Moving Average Chart

The solid line in Figure 10.1 is a 4-day moving average; the dash represents a 9-day moving average; and the dots are an 18-day moving average. You can find the latest 40-day moving average figure in the lower right-hand corner of the information box.

FIGURE 10.2   Example of a 40-Day Moving Average Chart

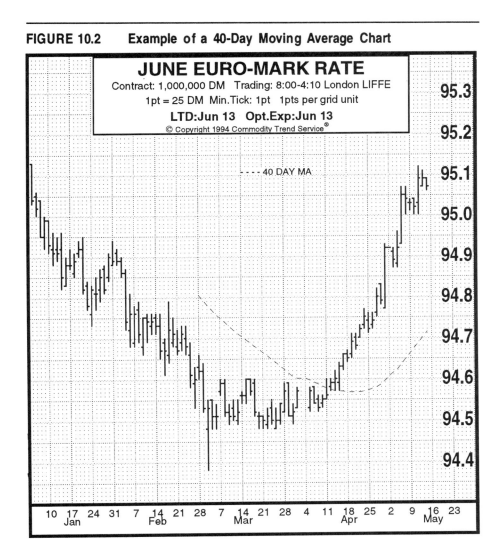

JUNE EURO-MARK RATE
Contract: 1,000,000 DM   Trading: 8:00-4:10 London LIFFE
1pt = 25 DM   Min.Tick: 1pt   1pts per grid unit
LTD:Jun 13   Opt.Exp:Jun 13
© Copyright 1994 Commodity Trend Service®

Forty-day moving average charts, such as the one shown in Figure 10.2, are very useful, since these 40-day lines tend to reflect support and resistance lines. It is a quick indication as to where a contract will meet buying or selling pressures.

CROSSOVER

The success of using moving averages can be summed up in one word—*crossover.* The crossover method looks at when different moving averages move over each other. Crossovers can provide both buy and sell signals.

FIGURE 10.3 Examples of Buy/Sell Crossover Signals

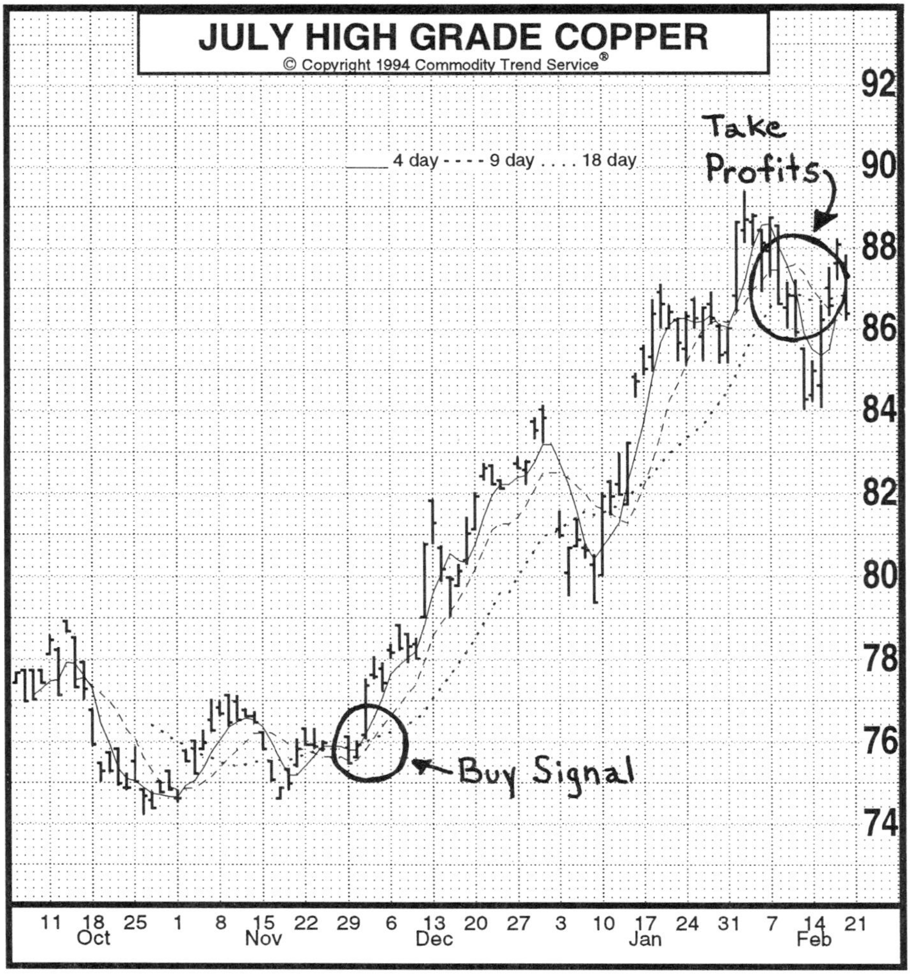
JULY HIGH GRADE COPPER
© Copyright 1994 Commodity Trend Service®
____ 4 day - - - - 9 day . . . . 18 day
Take Profits
Buy Signal
92
90
88
86
84
82
80
78
76
74
11 18 25 1 8 15 22 29 6 13 20 27 3 10 17 24 31 7 14 21
Oct Nov Dec Jan Feb

A buy signal is generated when a 4-day moving average moves above a 9-day and the 9-day moving average is above the 18-day line. All three must be increasing.

A sell signal occurs when a 4-day moving average moves below a 9-day and the 9-day is also below the 18-day moving average. All three must be decreasing. Figures 10.3 and 10.4 show examples of buy and sell crossover signals.

FIGURE 10.4   Another Example of Buy/Sell Crossover Signals

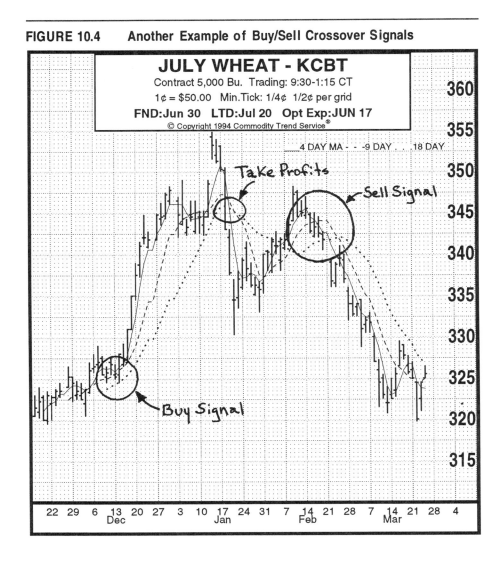

FACTORS TO CONSIDER

While moving averages can be a very useful tool, keep their strengths and benefits in perspective.

Here are five suggestions to consider when using moving averages:

1. If you get a buy or sell signal and you take on a position, keep that position until the 18-day line goes flat or changes direction. Do not take on a new position until there is a proper realignment of all three averages.
2. To protect accumulated profits along the way, use a trailing stop order—with the 40-day moving average as a stop point.
3. Think of the 40-day moving average as a support or resistance line.
4. Moving averages work very well in uptrends and downtrends and not as well in sideways markets. That's because in sideways markets, you can get buy signals near tops and sell signals near the bottom. If you trade on those signals, you will incur loss.
5. Because moving averages do not work that well in sideways markets—which can occur a fair amount of time—use caution. Look for markets that trend a great deal if you plan to rely on this tool.

YOU CAN DO IT

The examples in Figures 10.5–10.10 have a number of buy or sell opportunities. Mark where you would go long or short based on moving averages.

FIGURE 10.5   **YOU CAN DO IT**
Identify Buy or Sell Crossover Opportunities
(Moving Averages)
Number 1

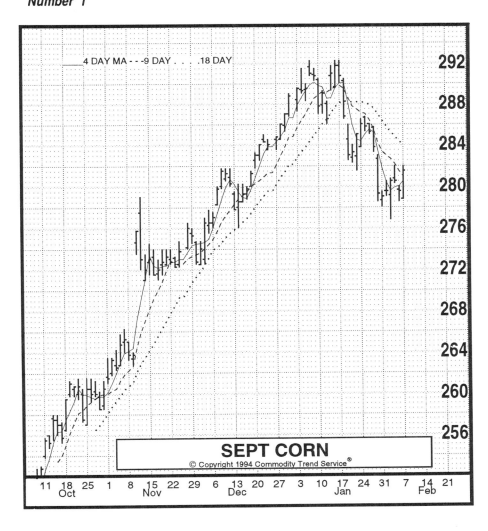

4 DAY MA - - -9 DAY . . . .18 DAY

SEPT CORN
© Copyright 1994 Commodity Trend Service®

FIGURE 10.6   **ANSWER**
Crossover Opportunities (Moving Averages)
Number 1

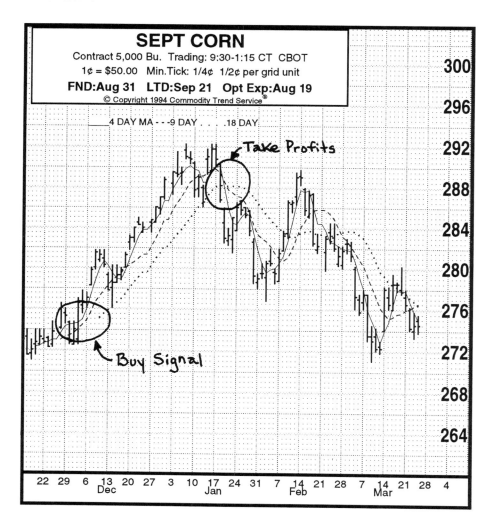

FIGURE 10.7   **YOU CAN DO IT**
Identify Buy or Sell Crossover Opportunities
(Moving Averages)
Number 2

FIGURE 10.8   ANSWER
Crossover Opportunities (Moving Averages)
Number 2

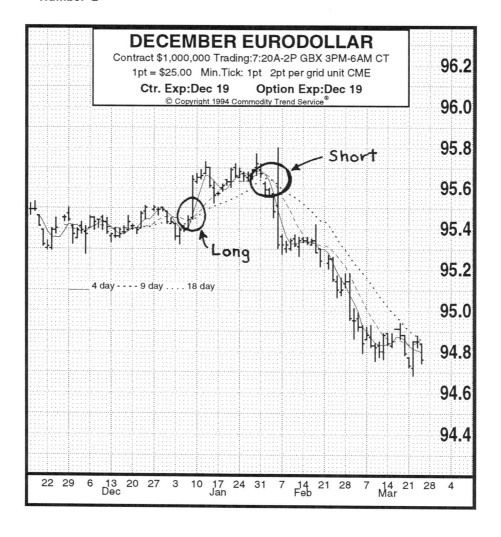

DECEMBER EURODOLLAR
Contract $1,000,000 Trading:7:20A-2P GBX 3PM-6AM CT
1pt = $25.00   Min.Tick: 1pt   2pt per grid unit CME
Ctr. Exp:Dec 19   Option Exp:Dec 19
© Copyright 1994 Commodity Trend Service®

FIGURE 10.9   **YOU CAN DO IT**
Identify Buy or Sell Crossover Opportunities
(Moving Averages)
Number 3

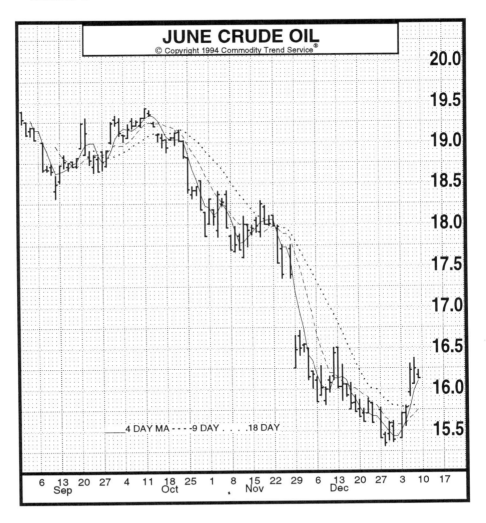

FIGURE 10.10　　**ANSWER**
Crossover Opportunities (Moving Averages)
Number 3

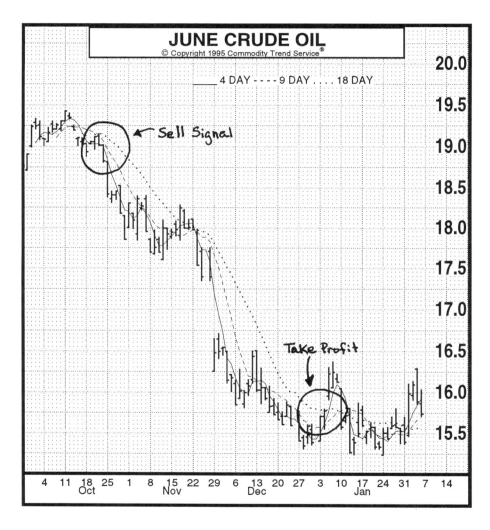

11 | WHAT OTHERS ARE DOING— MARKET SENTIMENT AND NET TRADER POSITIONS

Throughout this book, you have heard a repeating phrase: Trade in the direction of the primary trend. But as we also know, there are times when too many people on the bandwagon means it's time to get off.

This chapter will tell you how to find out what others are doing. That way, you can make better and more sophisticated decisions as to whether you want to be in or out of the market.

MARKET SENTIMENT

Market sentiment is a reflection of how bullish a universe of professional traders are on a particular futures instrument during any given time. You can find market sentiment numbers for the week in charting services such as in the *Futures Charts'* "Trend-Setter" table. On a historical basis, they are also plotted on numerous weekly charts. Figures 11.1 and 11.2 are examples of weekly market sentiment figures for financial and agricultural markets from *Futures Charts*. A chart plotting historical market sentiment for a sample commodity is shown in Figure 11.3.

FIGURE 11.1   Weekly Market Sentiment Figures—Financial Futures Markets

Commodity	Contract Month	Position	Position Established		Open Position		Closed* Profit/Loss	Market Sentiment
					Profit	Loss		
Copper	Sep 94	Long	04/18	8760	5513		25	64%
Comex Gold	Aug 94	Short	07/07	3842		-90	-3050	53%
Platinum	Oct 94	Long	05/10	3975	340		-2575	51%
Silver	Sep 94	Short	06/23	5450	775		-110	47%
Euro $	Sep 94	Short	06/29	9468	150		1750	45%
T-Bills	Sep 94	Short	07/01	9512	100		2073	46%
T-Bonds	Sep 94	Short	06/16	10318	3000		5251	35%
Muni Bonds	Sep 94	Short	06/22	9020	1875		3934	42%
T-Notes	Sep 94	Short	06/22	10405	1531		1996	41%
Crude Oil	Aug 94	Long	04/05	1571	3770		510	64%
Heat Oil	Aug 94	Short	07/08	4830		-206	231	62%
Unlead Gas	Aug 94	Short	06/28	5315	155		609	60%
B-Pound	Sep 94	Long	04/15	14640	5263		-1964	61%
Canadian $	Sep 94	*Short					-330	45%
D-Mark	Sep 94	Long	06/16	6124	3413		-2877	70%
J-Yen	Sep 94	Long	06/08	9669	7163		762	63%
S-Franc	Sep 94	Long	04/20	6953	8113		-5515	70%
Dollar Ind	Sep 94	Short	06/14	9241	3360		-2880	36%

*Closed trades from Jan.1, 1994   Totals: 44223   -2160

The percentage bullish refers to the most current market sentiment figure. When market sentiment numbers are between approximately 30 percent and 70 percent, the existing price trend will most likely continue.

When market sentiment numbers climb above approximately 75 percent to 80 percent, prices are entering an overbought condition. An oversold condition exists when sentiment numbers are below 20 percent to 25 percent. When the prices are overbought or oversold, it is time to consider taking a contrarian position.

FIGURE 11.2   Weekly Market Sentiment Figures—Agricultural Markets

Commodity	Contract Month	Position	Position Established		Open Position Profit	Loss	Closed* Profit/Loss	Market Sentiment
Corn	Dec 94	Short	06/21	2540	1313		2499	44%
Oats	Sep 94	Short	06/23	1260	413		-954	41%
Soybeans	Nov 94	Short	06/22	6520	3200		-3652	45%
Bean Meal	Dec 94	Short	06/29	1910	1020		-1500	46%
Bean Oil	Dec 94	Short	06/21	2670	1818		1296	43%
Wheat	Dec 94	Short	06/21	3370	238		-2538	42%
KC Wheat	Sep 94	Short	06/21	3300	75		1250	42%
Cocoa	Sep 94	Long	07/08	1386	35		535	58%
Coffee	Sep 94	Long	03/07	8030	40519		-2308	76%
O. Juice	Sep 94	Short	03/30	11590	2805		-1201	29%
Sugar	Oct 94	Short	06/23	1187	616		-1470	51%
Cotton	Dec 94	Short	06/28	7345	835		3105	44%
Lumber	Sep 94	Short	06/16	3800	5344		-4400	43%
L Cattle	Aug 94	*Long					-1220	39%
F Cattle	Aug 94	Long	07/05	7535	750		-900	43%
L Hogs	Aug 94	Short	06/23	4610	1000		-780	31%
Bellies	Aug 94	Short	06/24	3880	1480		-6900	31%

*Closed trades from Jan.1, 1994   Totals: 61459   -19138

Every instrument is overbought or oversold at some time or other, but the percentage numbers may fluctuate. You get a clearer picture when the charts show you three to four years' worth of market sentiment figures. By examining these charts, you can see what market sentiment numbers typically mark tops and bottoms over the past few years. Thus, they provide you with the best guide for judging the current market sentiment.

FIGURE 11.3 Example of Plotted Historical Market Sentiment

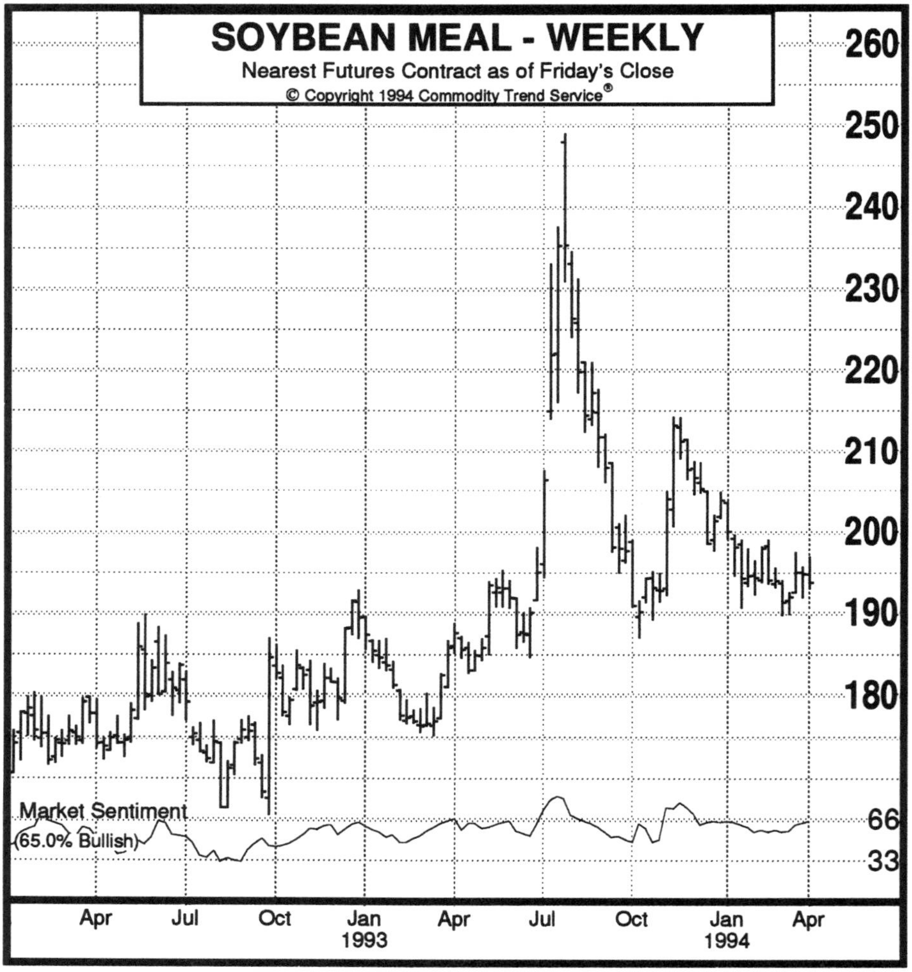
SOYBEAN MEAL - WEEKLY
Nearest Futures Contract as of Friday's Close
© Copyright 1994 Commodity Trend Service®
260
250
240
230
220
210
200
190
180
Market Sentiment
(65.0% Bullish)
66
33
Apr
Jul
Oct
Jan
1993
Apr
Jul
Oct
Jan
1994
Apr

YOU
CAN
DO IT

In Figures 11.4–11.7, circle and mark those times when sentiment figures indicated that the market was overbought or oversold. Compare those times to the actual price movements of the futures instrument.

FIGURE 11.4   **YOU CAN DO IT**
Identify Overbought and Oversold Conditions
(Market Sentiment)
Number 1

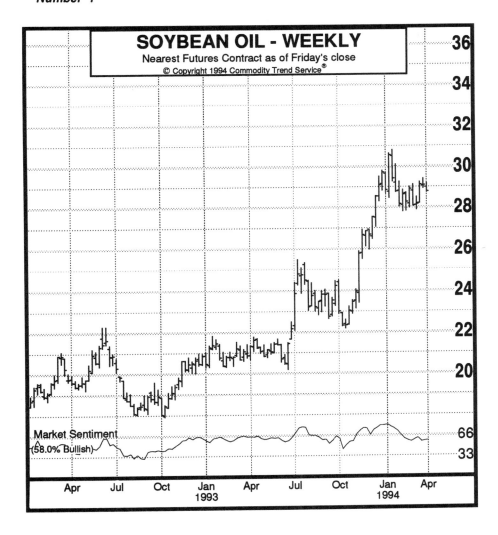

FIGURE 11.5   **ANSWER**
Overbought and Oversold Conditions (Market Sentiment)
Number 1

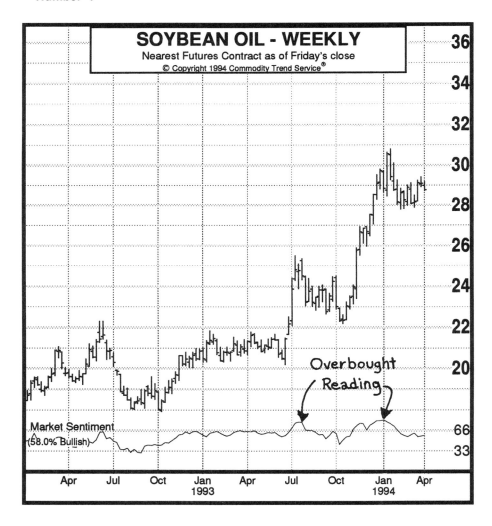

FIGURE 11.6   **YOU CAN DO IT**
Identify Overbought and Oversold Conditions
(Market Sentiment)
Number 2

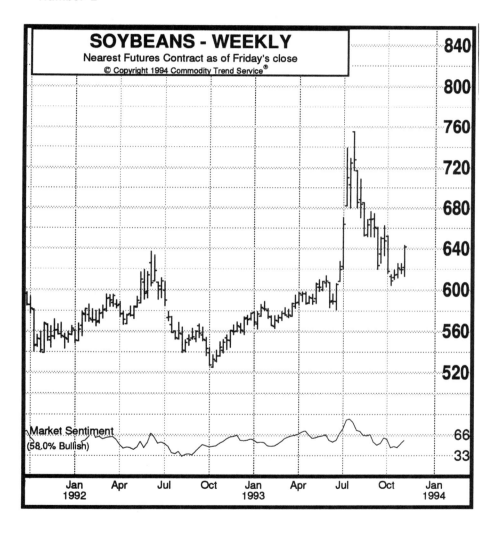

FIGURE 11.7   ANSWER
Overbought and Oversold Conditions (Market Sentiment)
Number 2

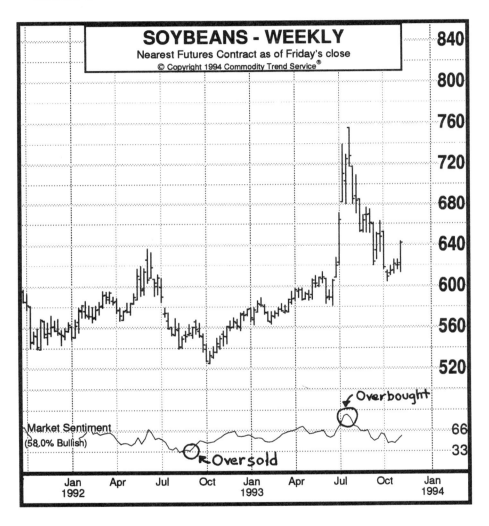

NET TRADER POSITIONS

While market sentiment gives you an indication of what professional traders feel, that is not the same as putting money on the line. There is a great difference between talk and action.

To help you really see how traders are investing, the *net trader position* charts provide an accurate portrait of how three key trading groups are acting in the market.

Twice a month, the Commodity Futures Trading Commission (CFTC) issues a report showing the positions (i.e., open interest) of three trading groups:

1. *The commercial traders.* These are the large hedgers—the companies that are involved in the actual commodity. They register as hedgers, because then they are entitled to lower margin requirements.

   Hedgers are interested in locking in prices and protecting themselves from major price fluctuations. Because they are involved with the commodity, they are very close to the fundamentals and are considered the "smart money." They are usually well financed and are in the business for the long haul.

2. *Large speculators.* These are, primarily, the world commodity funds, who rely heavily on a trend-following approach. They are well financed, conduct a large number of trades and provide liquidity to the market. In contrast to the hedger, who is motivated by protection, the large speculator is motivated by greed. And greed and clear thinking don't always go hand in hand.

3. *Small traders.* The CFTC keeps track of commercials and large speculators. Everyone else is lumped into the small trader category.

   It is unfortunate, but usually true small speculators represent the general uninformed public. For the most part, small speculators don't have the understanding of the futures market and the discipline required. That's why most of them buy at the top and sell at the bottom. Probably less than 10 percent of them are technically oriented and have the discipline to sell when other small speculators are buying. By practicing the skills you are learning in this book, you can distance yourself from the uninformed trader.

To recap, the large hedgers, or the *commercials,* as they are also called, have the best long-term track record. Large speculators have a respectable batting average, otherwise, new money would never flow into their funds. And small speculators, who are overleveraged and undercapitalized, have the worst track records. Figures 11.8 and 11.9 illustrate net trader positions.

In Figures 11.8 and 11.9, commercial hedgers are plotted as a solid line, large speculators are a dashed line and small speculators are the dotted line.

FIGURE 11.8   Example of Net Trader Positions
Number 1

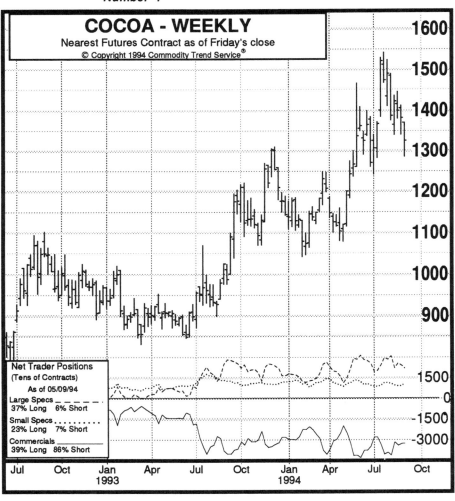

FIGURE 11.9   **Example of Net Trader Positions**
                  Number 2

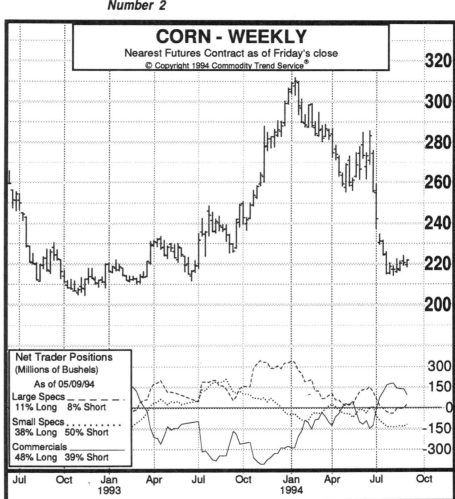

Every net trader position chart has three pairs of percentages. Let's analyze them.

Large speculators	15% Long	2% Short
Small speculators	43% Long	24% Short
Commercials	35% Long	66% Short

In this example, large speculators hold 15 percent of the total long positions in this particular market, while only holding 2 percent of the short positions. If you add all three long positions (93 percent) or all three short positions (92 percent), you do not usually get 100 percent, because spreading is not included in these net figures.

How are these percentages plotted on the chart? If, for example, small speculators were long 25,000 contracts and short 14,000 contracts, this would be plotted as +11,000. On the other hand, if commercials had 20,000 long contracts and 38,000 short contracts, their plot point would be -18,000.

Following are rules of thumb regarding net trader positions.

Rules of Thumb

- Small speculators are too bearish at bottoms and too bullish at tops.

- Large speculators usually are on the right side of major moves.

- And finally, watch the movement of commercials. They are well financed and have a strong economic reason for maintaining their positions. You'll find that they are sellers at major tops and buyers at major bottoms.

<table>
<tr><td>

YOU
CAN
DO IT

</td><td>

In Figures 11.10–11.15, you are going to make a buy or sell decision. We will show you a chart as of a given day. Examine the net trader positions and decide if you will go long or short on the last day of the chart. The answers will show you how the market reacted over the next few days or weeks.

</td></tr>
</table>

FIGURE 11.10   **YOU CAN DO IT**
Choose a Long or Short Position (Net Trader Positions)
Number 1

_____ Long   _____ Short

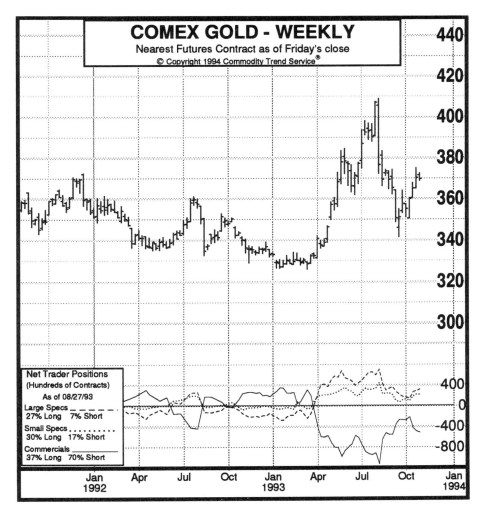

The commercial traders were holding a huge net short position (indicating the smart money perceived the market was overvalued). Additionally, large speculators were holding their largest net long position in years. This shows excessive speculation and underscores caution. From August through September, the market dropped 8 percent.

FIGURE 11.11   **ANSWER**
Net Trader Positions
Number 1

_____ **Long**   ✓ **Short**

FIGURE 11.12   **YOU CAN DO IT**

Choose a Long or Short Position (Net Trader Positions)
Number 2

_____   **Long**   _____   **Short**

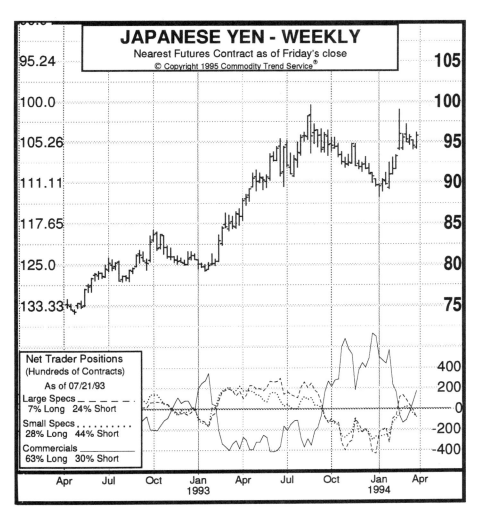

FIGURE 11.13   **ANSWER**
Net Trader Positions
Number 2

✓ **Long**   _____ **Short**

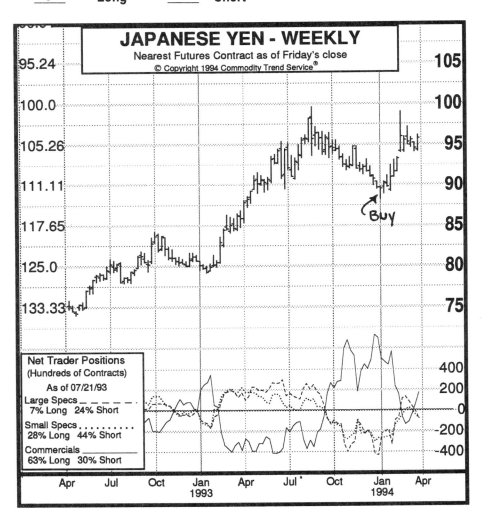

JAPANESE YEN - WEEKLY
Nearest Futures Contract as of Friday's close
© Copyright 1994 Commodity Trend Service®

Net Trader Positions
(Hundreds of Contracts)
As of 07/21/93
Large Specs _ _ _ _ _ .
7% Long 24% Short
Small Specs . . . .
28% Long 44% Short
Commercials _____
63% Long 30% Short

FIGURE 11.14   Net Trader Positions
Number 3

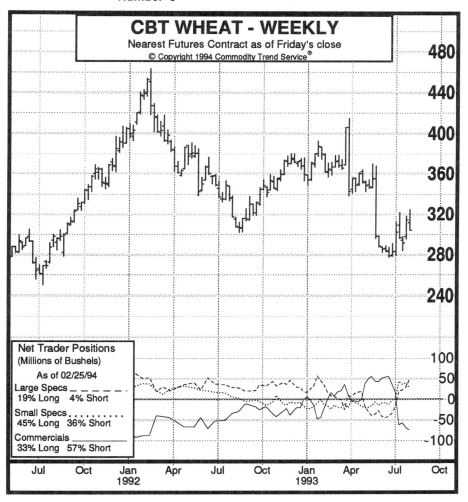

FIGURE 11.15   Net Trader Positions
                     Number 4

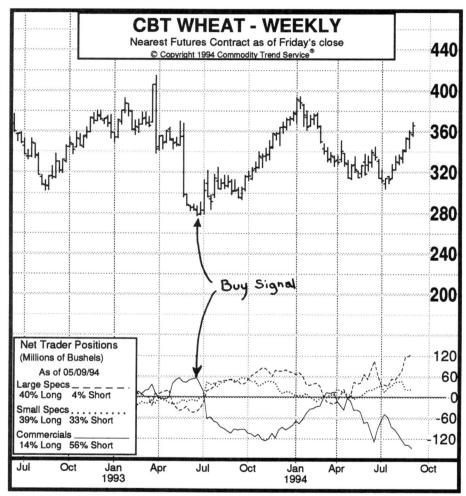

12 | EVERYTHING REPEATS— CYCLES

The concept of cycles is not new. It is reflected in our heritage, our language and our understanding of the seasons. The biblical story describes seven years of feast and seven years of famine. "What comes around, goes around" is a common expression. Intuitively, we believe that everything repeats.

Back in 1940, Edward Dewey organized the Foundation for the Study of Cycles, and it's still in operation today. That foundation, along with other leading economists and theoreticians, have done some fascinating work on this topic. This chapter reveals their findings and ways you can benefit from them.

CYCLES

A *cycle* is a repetitive sequence of events. In the world of commodities, you're apt to find a number of cycles—the most common being the following:

- *Long-term cycles* can run from two years to ten years and sometimes well beyond that.
- *Seasonal cycles* run a year. Take corn, for example, which is a summer crop—planted in the spring and harvested in the fall. Prices are generally low at harvesttime, when supplies are abundant, and then tend to rise in the spring, just before a new crop is planted.

- *Primary* or *intermediate cycles* can run from two to six months.
- *Short-term trading cycles,* which can run about 28–30 days, are very prevalent and very important.

Cycles are a time projection—not a price projection. That is why you will not see a price scale alongside a cycle chart.

How are cycles drawn? Cycles are projected forward for a period that is most likely to contain a cyclical high and low. The projected period for the cycle low is generally more accurate than the cycle high projection. Once a cycle high and low have been confirmed, the cycle is redrawn to match actual highs and lows.

As you look at a cycle graph, you cannot help but notice that the tops often point in different directions (see Figures 12.1 and 12.2). After all, you might expect that if you had a 30-day cycle, the high would come at the midpoint on the 15th day. But cycles are seldom symmetrical. They react differently in bull and bear markets.

In a bull market, the crest or apex of the cycle leans to the right, because the highs are to the right of the cycle's midpoint. This is called a *right translation.* In strong bull markets, cycle lengths tend to contract (shorten) slightly.

Look for just the opposite in bear markets. The cycles tend to be slightly longer than they were in bull markets. Cycles in bear markets tend to peak early—to the left of the midpoint. When the apex is to the left of the mid-point, the cycle is called a *left translation.*

What do professional traders look for when they use cycles? They are looking for consistency. A series of right translations in a long-term primary uptrend is reassuring. However, if we are in such an uptrend and we begin to see a shift to a left translation, it's usually an early sign that the trend is changing.

Because cycles can help us predict changes in the primary trend, they are considered *leading indicators,* as opposed to moving averages, which are considered *trailing indicators.*

FIGURE 12.1 Examples of Cycles

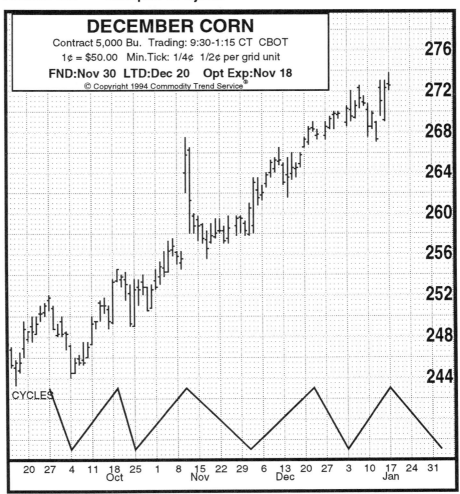

Experts agree that if the distance between cycle lows has been consistent (that is, approximately the same width from valley to valley), cycles can be used for market timing. However, if the cycles have been irregular, it's best to use other tools to type your trades.

FIGURE 12.2   Another Example of Cycles

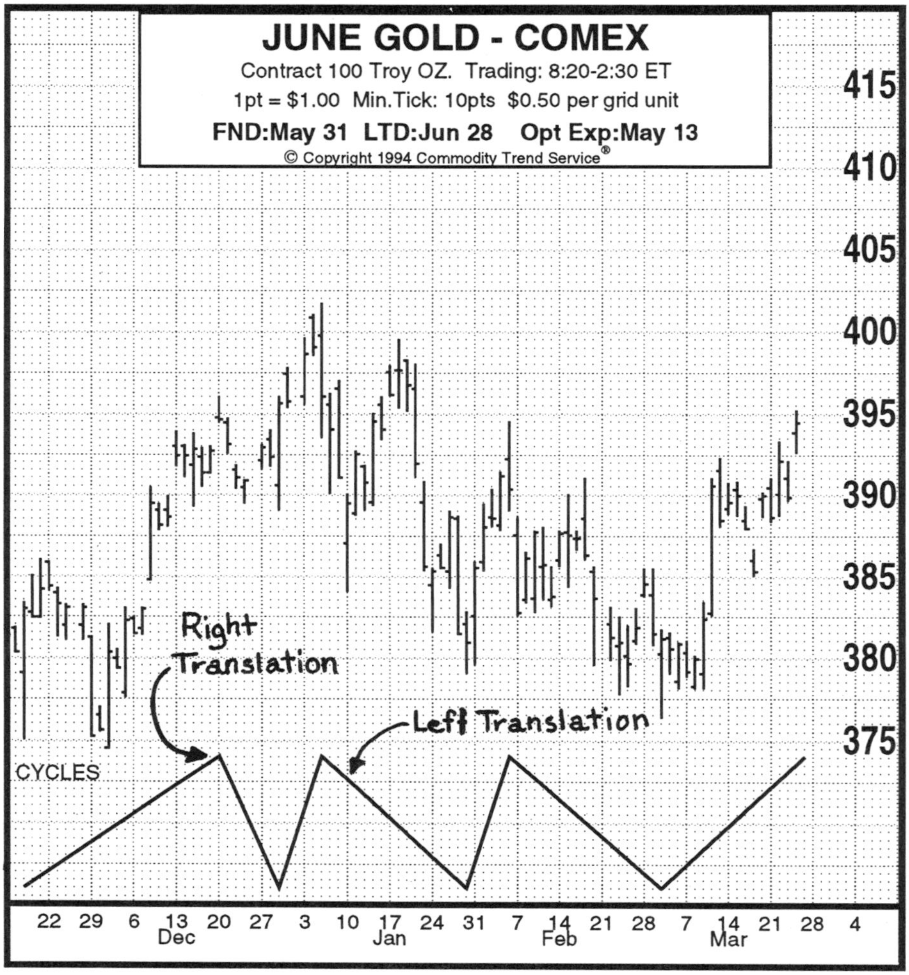

YOU
CAN
DO IT

Here's a chance to get comfortable with cycles. In Figures 12.3–12.8, you will find both left and right translations. Mark the peaks "LT" or "RT," as appropriate.

FIGURE 12.3   YOU CAN DO IT
Identify the Cycles
Number 1

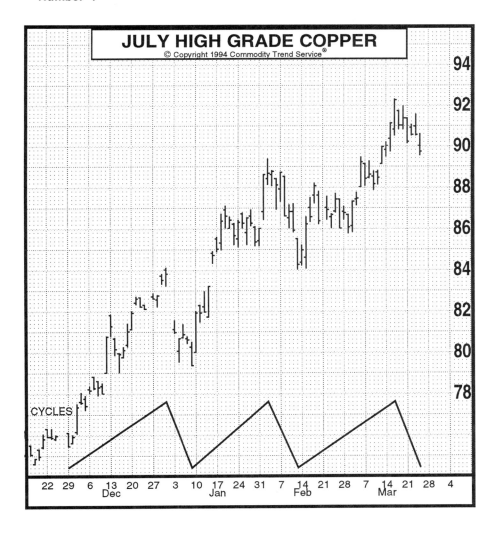

FIGURE 12.4   ANSWER
Cycles
Number 1

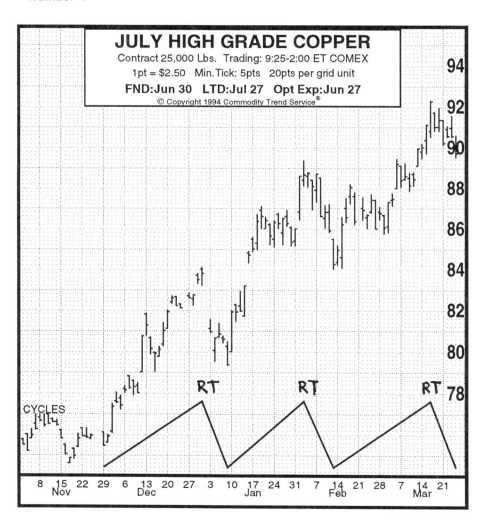

FIGURE 12.5 **YOU CAN DO IT**
Identify the Cycles
Number 2

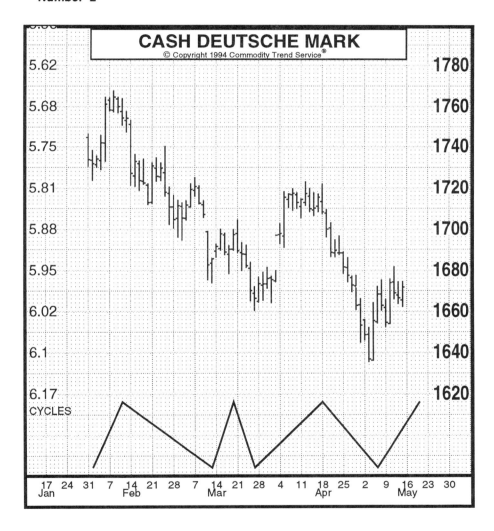

FIGURE 12.6   **ANSWER**
Cycles
Number 2

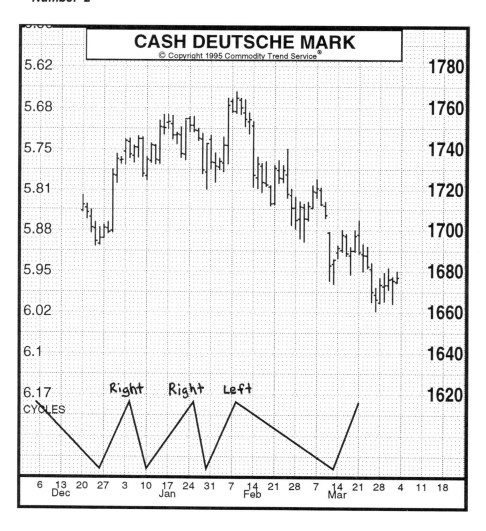

FIGURE 12.7 **YOU CAN DO IT**
Identify the Cycles
Number 3

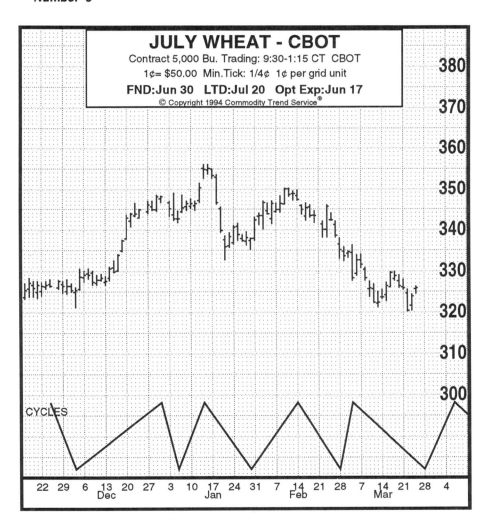

FIGURE 12.8   **ANSWER**
Cycles
Number 3

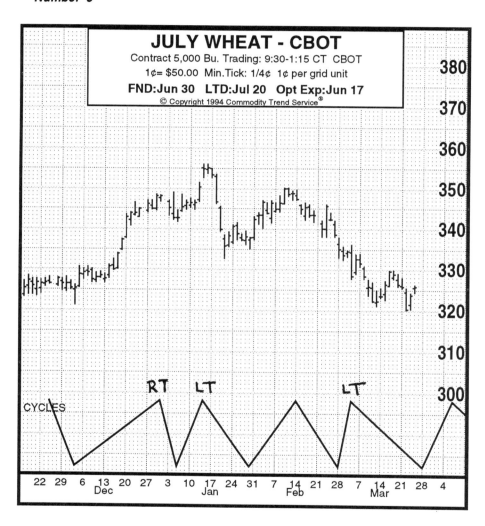

13

A Winning Pair of Leading Indicators— Cash and Spreads

Some technical indicators are based on sophisticated formulas, which make it difficult for some investors to understand and appreciate them. On the other hand, some indicators are based on simple computations—and they work well. Cash and spreads are two such indicators.

CASH

For every commodity future, activity is occurring in two markets all the time: the cash or spot market and the futures market.

In the *cash* market, the commodity physically trades hands: e.g., between a farmer and a food processor or between an oil producer and an oil distributor. Cash prices respond to supply and demand for the actual commodity.

On the other hand, futures prices react to traders' expectations. And while these two prices are similar, they rarely are exactly the same.

Why is cash a leading indicator, especially for nearby months? Because at expiration, we expect cash and futures prices to come together. After all, at expiration, a futures contract can be settled by the actual commodity, so their prices have to be on a par with each other.

If cash is higher than the futures market, we expect that gap to narrow as we get closer to expiration, as illustrated in Figure 13.1. Notice how futures prices constantly moved up to cash. As you can see, futures prices generally will rise to cash prices and narrow the basis.

On the other hand, if cash is below futures (as it is in Figure 13.2), you might want to be in a short position as futures will tend to drop, assuming no major disruption to the actual commodity market.

All in all, cash is an excellent indicator.

SPREADS

A *spread* is the purchase and sale of two contracts in the same commodity or economically related commodities.

For example, going long March sugar contracts and simultaneously going short May sugar contracts would be considered a spread. Another spread example would be going short September Eurodollars and going long September T-bills, since both of these commodities are economically related.

Why do investors engage in spreads? Because it minimizes their risk exposure. For example, they may be bullish and therefore may take on the long position. But by also taking on a short position, they can minimize losses if prices move down.

Here is an example of a spread. In January, a trader purchases May copper at $1.08 and sells July copper at $1.07½. Three months later, copper rises in price. He liquidates his long May position at 1.12 and offsets his July contract at 1.11. Our trader made a gain of 4 cents on his long position and had a loss of 3½ cents on his short position, for a net gain of .5 cents, or $125 per contract—all done with minimum exposure to our trader.

Types of Spreads

There are two types of spreads: a bull spread and a bear spread. A *bull spread* is the purchase of a nearby contract and going short the distant contract. When we say that a bull spread is strengthening, we see the nearby months rising

FIGURE 13.1   Example of Cash above Future Prices

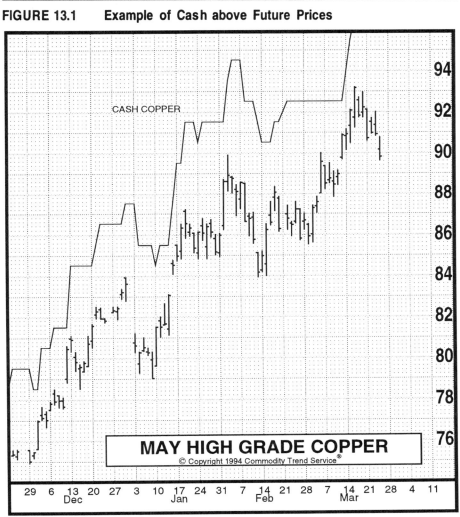

faster than the distant months, indicating an increased demand for the commodity.

A *bear spread* is the short sale of a nearby month and the taking on of a long position in a distant month. An overabundance of a commodity may thereby weaken the prices in the nearby month. That's why investors would short the nearby and go long the distant month.

FIGURE 13.2   Example of Cash below Futures

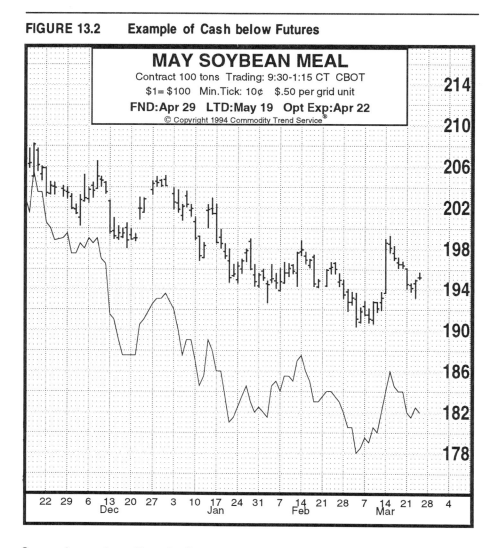

Spreads as Leading Indicators

Professional traders use spreads as a leading indicator by tracking the relationship of nearby and distant months of the same commodity or economically related commodities.

Fortunately, charts can do all the tracking work for you. Spread charts that are right on the same page as the actual commodity enable you to see the true relationship of spreads and prices.

FIGURE 13.3   Example of Spreads

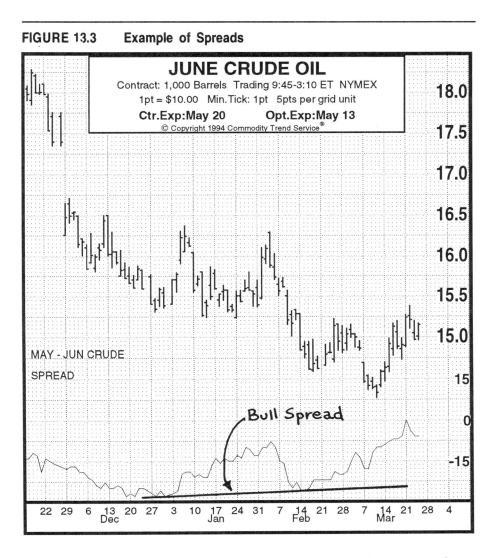

In Figure 13.3, we see a bull spread, which generally precedes an upward correction. This is considered a technical divergence.

Keep in mind this rule of thumb: Spreads are an excellent leading indicator, especially for bull markets, but *they really work best when they deal with a physical commodity of limited supply,* including metals, grains and meats. Consequently, they are not as effective for financial instrument contracts or options.

YOU CAN DO IT

In Figures 13.4–13.9, you are going to make a buy, sell or no-action decision. We will show you a chart as of a given day. Examine the cash and spread charts and decide if you will go long or short or decide to take no action. Compare your decisions with how the market reacted.

FIGURE 13.4   YOU CAN DO IT
Choose Long, Short or No Action (Cash and Spreads)
Number 1

_____ **Long**   _____ **Short**   _____ **No Action**

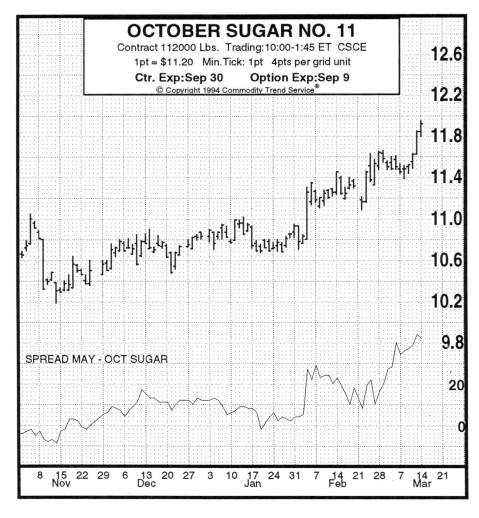

OCTOBER SUGAR NO. 11
Contract 112000 Lbs. Trading: 10:00-1:45 ET CSCE
1pt = $11.20 Min. Tick: 1pt 4pts per grid unit
Ctr. Exp: Sep 30   Option Exp: Sep 9
© Copyright 1994 Commodity Trend Service®

SPREAD MAY - OCT SUGAR

FIGURE 13.5 **ANSWER**
Cash and Spreads
Number 1

✓ ____ Long   ____ Short   ____ No Action

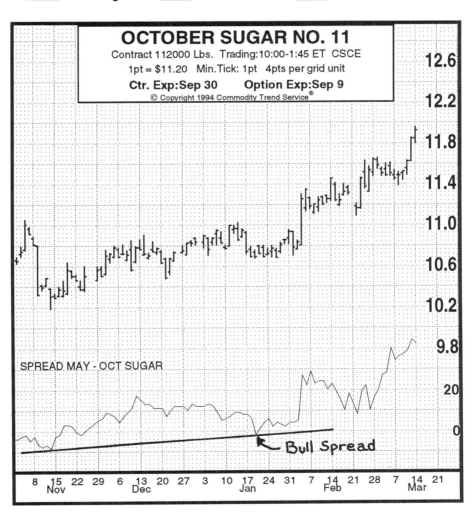

FIGURE 13.6   **YOU CAN DO IT**
Choose Long, Short or No Action (Cash and Spreads)
Number 2

_____ **Long**   _____ **Short**   _____ **No Action**

FIGURE 13.7   **ANSWER**
Cash and Spreads
Number 2

_____ Long   ✓ Short   _____ No Action

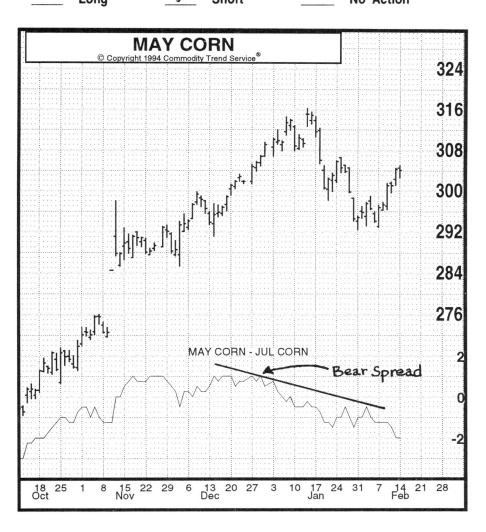

FIGURE 13.8   YOU CAN DO IT
Choose Long, Short or No Action (Cash and Spreads)
Number 3

_____ **Long**   _____ **Short**   _____ **No Action**

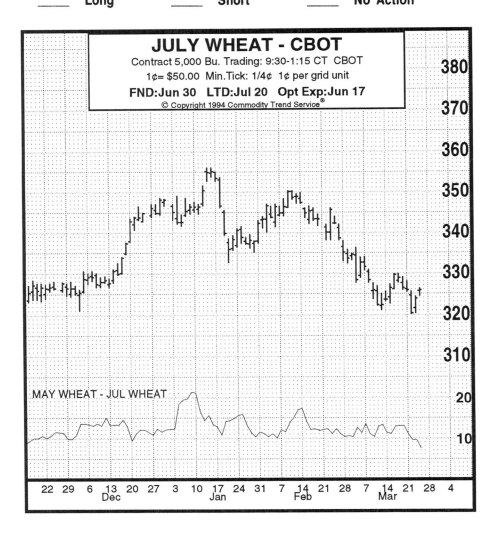

FIGURE 13.9   **ANSWER**
Cash and Spreads
Number 3

_____ **Long**   _____ **Short**   ✓ **No Action**

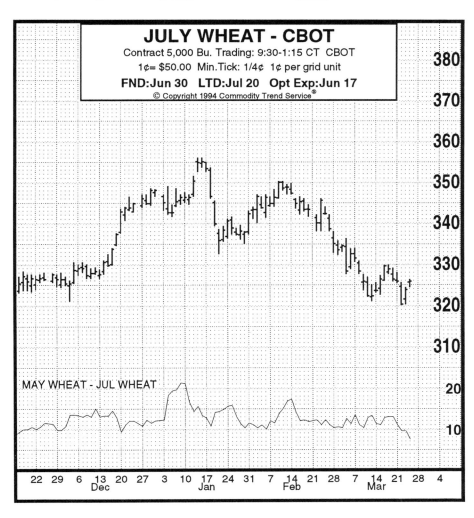

JULY WHEAT - CBOT
Contract 5,000 Bu. Trading: 9:30-1:15 CT CBOT
1¢= $50.00 Min.Tick: 1/4¢ 1¢ per grid unit
FND:Jun 30   LTD:Jul 20   Opt Exp:Jun 17
© Copyright 1994 Commodity Trend Service®

MAY WHEAT - JUL WHEAT

<table>
<tr><td>**14**</td><td># MOVING WITH MOMENTUM—
RELATIVE STRENGTH INDEX</td></tr>
</table>

Momentum is an amazing phenomenon. When a market starts building momentum, people start jumping on the bandwagon. Of course, like any natural phenomenon, momentum dissipates. Professional traders know how to read the charts to determine if a trend is losing momentum. This chapter will show you how to get off the bandwagon before everyone else does and certainly before a stampede.

Momentum is a basic component of a series of technical analysis tools called oscillators. This chapter, as well as Chapters 15 and 16, address the major three oscillators.

MOMENTUM

Momentum is the rate of change of prices over a period of time, as opposed to the actual prices themselves.

Momentum is easy to compute. You take the closing price today, subtract the closing price ten days ago and then plot it. This assumes you are working on a ten-day chart. You cannot simply choose any number of days you want.

In the example shown in Figure 14.1, today's sugar is 9.30 cents per pound and ten days ago it was 8.80 cents per pound. The difference is .50 and we plot it. Next day, the closing price is 9.35 cents and ten days ago the closing

FIGURE 14.1   Example of Plotting Momentum

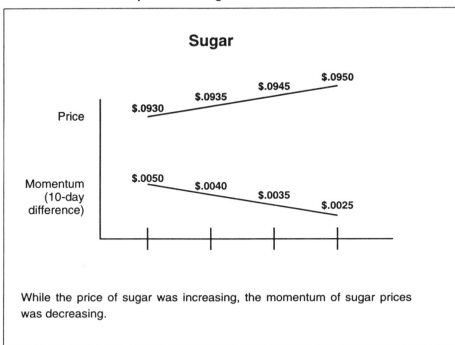

While the price of sugar was increasing, the momentum of sugar prices was decreasing.

price was 8.95 cents. The difference is .40 and we plot that. The third day, sugar is at 9.45 cents and ten days ago it was 9.10 cents. We plot the difference of .35. The fourth day sugar is at 9.50 cents per pound and ten days ago it was 9.25 cents per pound. Again, we plot the difference of .25.

Notice how in the example, sugar prices went up every day, giving the impression of a strong upward trend. But momentum figures were going down, indicating that perhaps sugar's upward trend was about to run its course and collapse.

Not all momentum charts use this type of scale, that is to say the difference between prices. The scale can be a percentage. The important thing to note is that they show the rate of change and not prices.

RELATIVE STRENGTH INDEX

One of the great technical analysts, J. Welles Wilder, developed the relative strength index (RSI) because of two limitations that a traditional momentum chart has. First, a radical movement ten days ago (in a ten-day chart) could cause a major fluctuation, which could give off an erroneous signal. Second, without a constant set of scales, it's hard to compare momentum over a long period.

What Wilder did was develop a formula that "evened out" sharp price movements and created a constant range of 0 to 100, thus solving both problems.

The relative strength index can warn you when a market is near a top or bottom. It all depends on whether it is in the overbought or oversold section of the chart and whether you have a bullish or bearish divergence.

Divergence

A *divergence* is a situation where a price line and an oscillator line (like the RSI) begin to diverge and start to move in opposite directions. This is a telltale sign that a trend line may be nearing a close and may change directions.

For example, in Figure 14.2 the price trend line is upward, yet the RSI chart is moving down. This is known as a *bearish divergence.*

Conversely, we see a *bullish divergence* in Figure 14.3 where the price trend line is downward, but the RSI has an upward slope.

Although divergences are important in analyzing oscillators, their usefulness is not limited exclusively to oscillators. As a case in point, if prices are rising and volume is falling, you have a bearish divergence—and a possible indication that prices will begin to pull back.

In an uptrending market with prices making new highs, an RSI climbing above 70 (the overbought area) warns of a trend reversal if the RSI peaks below its previous high. This is a bearish divergence. The reversal is confirmed when the RSI drops below its previous low. When an RSI's failure to make a new high is followed by a drop below its previous low, it is also called a *failure swing.*

FIGURE 14.2   Example of RSI and Bearish Divergence

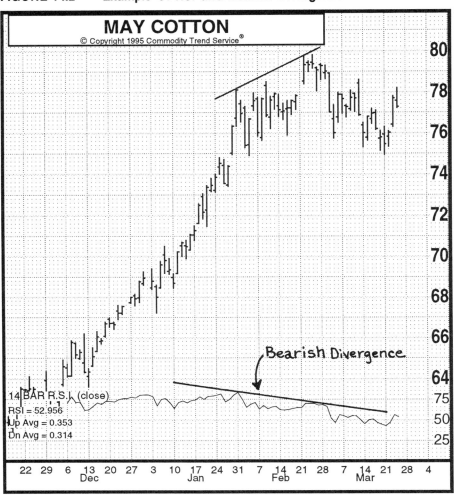

When the RSI dips below 30, it is in an oversold area. As prices move lower, we look to see if the RSI is moving up. We measure valley to valley, and if the second low is higher than the previous valley, we have a bullish divergence. Here again, the reversal is confirmed when the RSI rises above its previous peak.

In strong trending markets, the RSI may stay at an extreme level for an extended period. When the RSI reversals occur at these extremes, they are generally considered to be better signals.

FIGURE 14.3   Example of RSI and Bullish Divergence

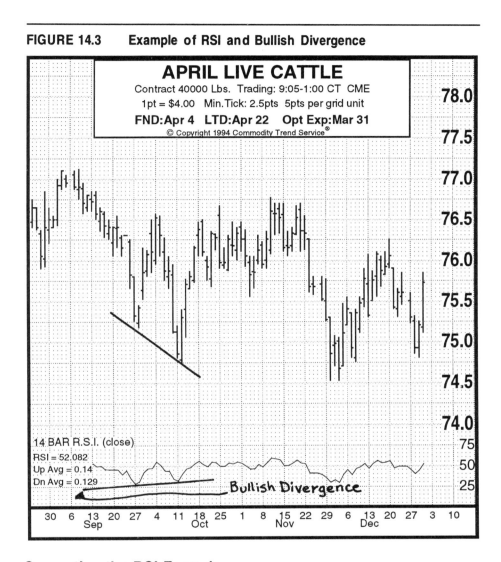

Computing the RSI Formula

Charts that plot the RSI for you every week are useful. At times, you might also want to keep track of the RSI on a daily basis—especially in volatile markets. You can do this easily with a simple calculator.

Here is the primary formula for the RSI:

$$\textbf{RSI} = \textbf{100} \times \frac{\textbf{U}}{\textbf{U} + \textbf{D}}$$

U = Up average
D = Down average

In the chart's information box, you will find the up average and down average, as of the publication date. To incorporate the new day's price change, use this simple three-step approach:

1. Determine if the current close is higher or lower than the previous close.
2. If the current close is higher, compute a new up average. If it is down, compute a new down average.
   ▮ Multiply the prior average (from step one) by 13.
   ▮ Add the daily net change (the new day's up or down amount).
   ▮ Divide the result by 14.
3. If the current close is higher than the previous close, use the new up average in the primary formula for the RSI. On the other hand, if the current close is lower than the previous close, use the new down average in the primary formula for the RSI.

Example

On February 7, sugar closed at 9.15 cents per pound. The information box in the chart read:

> 14 Bar RSI = 67.777
> Up average = 0.082
> Dn average = 0.039

On February 8, sugar closed at 9.25 cents per pound.

1. Determine whether the current close is higher or lower than the previous close.
2. If the current close is higher, as it is in this example, then you only need to compute a new up average.

▮ Multiply the prior up average by 13:

$$\text{Up average} = 13 \times .082 = 1.066$$

▮ Add the daily net change (the new day's up or down amount).

$$\text{Daily net change} = 9.25 - 9.15 = .10$$
$$\text{Up average} = 1.066 + .10 = 1.166$$

▮ Divide the result by 14:

$$\text{Up average} = 1.166 \div 14 = 0.083$$

3. Proceed with the primary formula using the new up average:

$$\text{RSI} = 100 \times \frac{0.083}{0.083 + 0.039} = 68.03$$

You Can Do It

Take out that calculator and compute the new day's RSI based on the information provided. On February 7, gold closed at $368.90 per troy ounce. The information box plotted in the chart read:

$$14 \text{ bar RSI} = 51.409$$
$$\text{Up average} = 1.150$$
$$\text{Dn average} = 1.087$$

On February 8, gold closed at $370.50 per troy ounce. Compute the new RSI:

1. Determine if the current close is higher or lower than the previous close.
2. Calculate the up or down average (circle one).
   ▮ Multiply the prior ___ average by 13: _____
   ▮ Add the daily net change (the new day's up or down amount): _____
   ▮ Divide the result by 14: _____
3. Proceed with the primary formula using the new ___ average: _____

The answer is **52.093** Use the up average for this example.

Step 2: $13 \times 1.150 = 14.95$
$14.95 + (370.50 - 368.90) = 16.55$
$16.55 \div 14 = 1.182$

Step 3: $100 \times (1.182 \div (1.182 + 1.087)) = 52.093$

┌─────────┐
│ **YOU** │   In the next two examples (see Figures 14.4–14.7), find the bullish or bearish
│ **CAN** │   divergences and label them as such. Also, indicate if you would go long,
│ **DO IT**│   short or take no action. Remember, RSI works best when it is in the over-
└─────────┘   bought or oversold areas.

FIGURE 14.4   **YOU CAN DO IT**
                     Chart the RSI Divergence
                     Number 1

_____ **Long**   _____ **Short**   _____ **No Action**

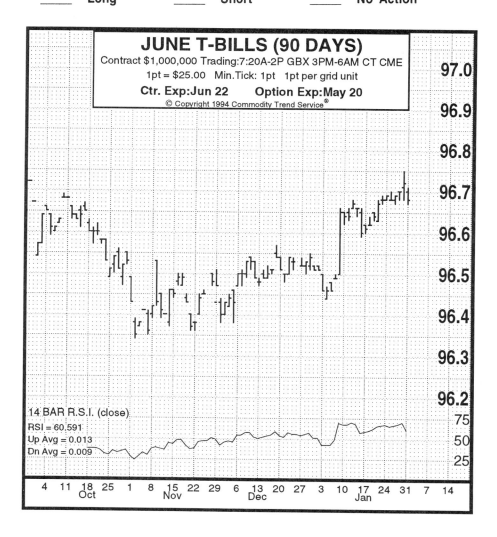

FIGURE 14.5 ANSWER
RSI Divergence
Number 1

_____ **Long**   ✓ **Short**   _____ **No Action**

FIGURE 14.6   **YOU CAN DO IT**
Chart the RSI Divergence
Number 2

_____ **Long**   _____ **Short**   _____ **No Action**

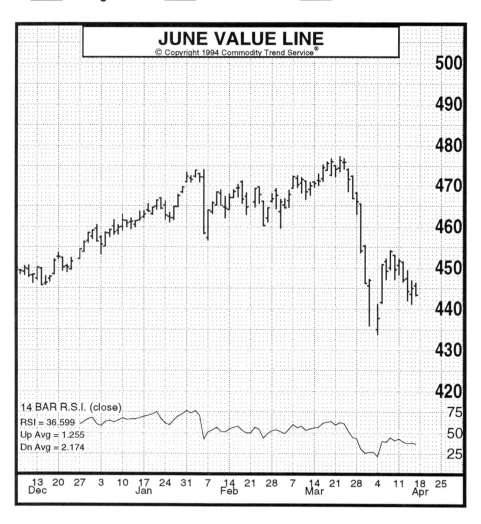

FIGURE 14.7   **ANSWER**
RSI Divergence
Number 2

_____   **Long**   ✓   **Short**   _____   **No Action**

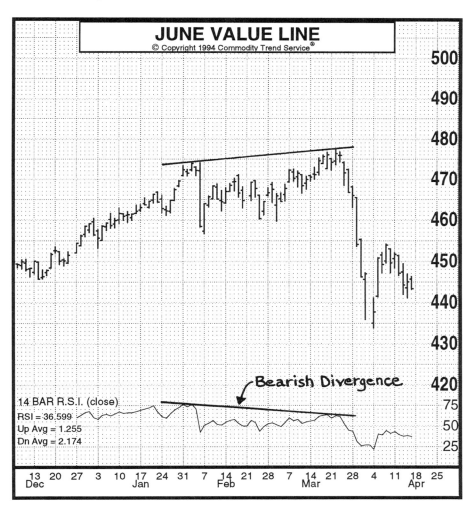

15 THE PROFESSIONAL'S TOOL— STOCHASTICS

Ask professional traders to name their top three technical analysis tools, and stochastics will be among them.

Stochastics is a powerful tool that takes some time to master. But once you have, it can help you trade profitably year after year.

STOCHASTICS

Stochastic values are functions of momentum, but from a more sophisticated point of view compared with other oscillators. They use the future's daily high, daily low and closing price.

The concept of stochastics is based on the tendency that as prices move higher, the daily close will be closer to the high of the daily range. The reverse is true in downtrends. As prices decrease, the daily close tends to move closer to the low of the daily range. This concept holds true for daily, weekly and monthly charts.

The charts in this chapter use a 14-bar time frame to compute stochastics. If you are working with a daily chart, each bar is a day. If you are examining a weekly chart, each bar is a week.

When the future's current price is near the top of the 14-bar range, stochastic numbers will be high. If prices are near the bottom of the 14-bar range, stochastic values will be low.

Stochastics is calculated using three sets of data: raw value, %K and %D. Initially, these may sound unusual; however, they are easily computed.

We will start with the raw value. It represents a relationship between the closing price and the range from high to low prices. Expressed as a formula, it is:

$$\text{Raw value} = 100 \times \frac{\text{Last close—14-Day low}}{\text{14-Day high—14-Day low}}$$

%K is a moving average of the raw value. It is considered a "fast stochastic," because it has many up and down swings over a very short period of time.

$$\text{New } \%K = 2/3 \text{ Previous } \%K + 1/3 \text{ New raw value}$$

%D is a three-day moving average of %K. The purpose of %D is to smooth the movement of %K, therefore the term "14-bar slow stochastic."

$$\text{New } \%D = 2/3 \text{ Previous } \%D + 1/3 \text{ New } \%K$$

In the sample charts in this chapter, %K is the dotted line and %D is the solid line.

Overbought and Oversold Areas

%K and %D are plotted on a scale from 0 to 100. Stochastic values above 75 indicate an overbought area—reflecting a market condition where prices have moved up and appear ready to correct.

Stochastic values below 25 indicate an oversold area—where prices have moved down and are poised to rebound.

Some professional traders prefer to use 80 and 20 as the parameters for overbought and oversold areas. You will develop your own guidelines as you use this tool. In sustained moves, stochastic values may remain in the overbought or oversold zones for an extended period.

Divergence

Like the RSI, stochastic lines may diverge with price to warn of a potential top or bottom. If prices make a new high, but the stochastics slope downward (with successive peaks being lower), a market top may be near.

Figure 15.1 is an example of bearish divergence and Figure 15.2 shows a bullish divergence.

FIGURE 15.1   Stochastics and Bearish Divergence

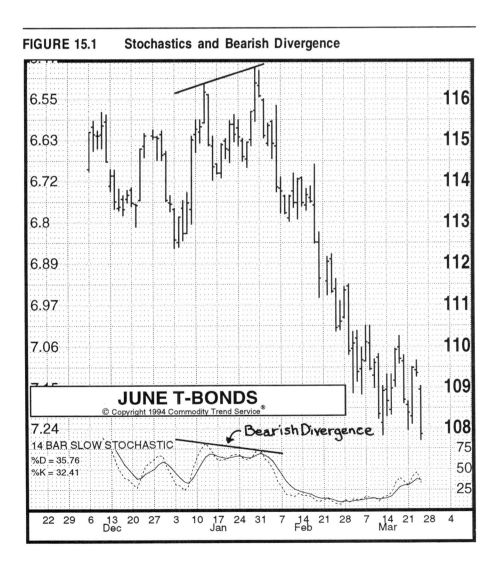

FIGURE 15.2   Stochastics and Bullish Divergence

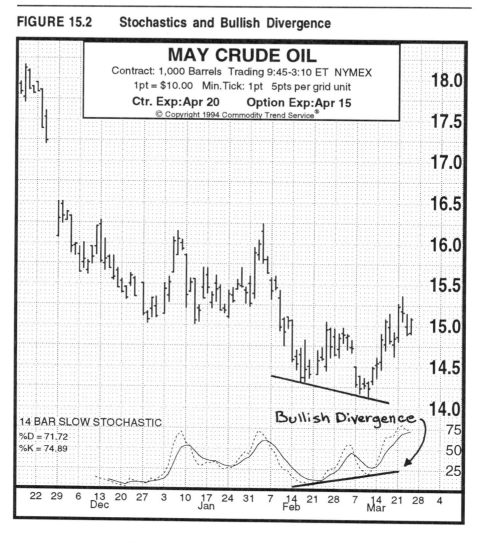

Don't expect to see divergence very often on long-term charts. It is much more common on daily charts.

On the other hand, viewing stochastics on weekly and monthly charts can be very useful for trend identification. With the help of stochastics, you can get a better sense of the long-term trend and trend changes. When both %K and %D are moving in the same direction, they confirm the existing trend. When the lines cross, especially after first rising above 75 or dropping below 25, they signal trend reversals. Knowing the long-term trend gives you confidence to trade in its primary direction.

Buy/Sell Signals

One reason professional traders rely on stochastic values is their ability to generate buy or sell signals. It occurs when the %K line (the dotted line) crosses the %D line (the solid line).

Before you learn the techniques, you need to put this approach in proper context. Studies have shown that making buy and sell decisions based solely on every time %K crossed %D produced poor to mediocre results. Stochastics by themselves do not constitute a trading system; instead, they are tools for you to use in making trading decisions. The key to using stochastics successfully is filtering out as many of the unprofitable signals as possible. Here are a couple of suggestions:

1. Both stochastic lines must be in the overbought or oversold zones before using a %K line crossing a %D line as a buy or sell signal.
2. Use stochastic signals only in the direction of the long-term trend. After referring to the monthly or weekly charts, follow buy signals on the daily stochastics charts in uptrends and sell signals in downtrends.

   For example, a futures market you have been following is trending up. Look for buy signals when stochastics are below 25. If you are looking for an exit point to take a profit, don't rely on just stochastics for sell signals in this uptrending market.

   On the other hand, if the market you are following is moving primarily downward and you want to go short, look for sell signals when stochastics is above 75.

More aggressive professional traders use all crossings in the direction of a major trend, regardless of where the stochastic lines cross. If you were to follow this aggressive approach in an uptrending market, you would take all the upturns by the daily stochastics as additional buy signals (e.g., to pyramid your positions), regardless of whether %K or %D reached the oversold zone. Stochastic sell signals are ignored, except to take short-term profits.

Conversely, in an aggressive posture in a downward market, you might see all downturn on the daily stochastics as signals to sell or pyramid short positions, even if %K or %D had not reached the overbought area. Stochastic buy signals are ignored, except to take short-term profits. Figure 15.3 gives you an example of buy/sell signals.

Because of their ability to help in market timing decisions, stochastics can be a vital tool in your arsenal. In time, it will no doubt be one of your top three technical analysis tools.

FIGURE 15.3   Example of Stochastic Buy/Sell Signals

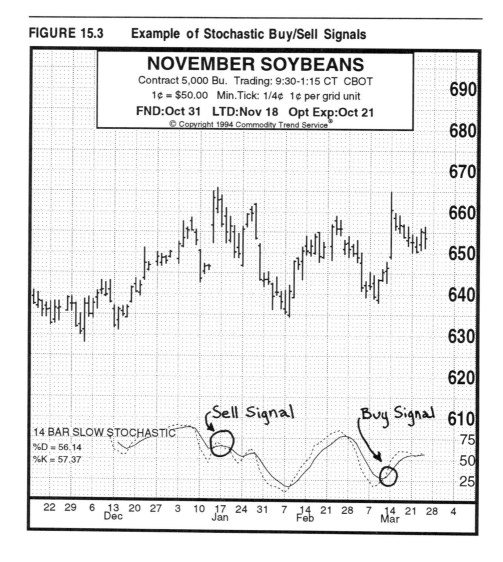

YOU CAN DO IT

In Figures 15.4–15.9, draw historic bullish and bearish divergence lines as you see them. Label them bullish or bearish.

FIGURE 15.4   YOU CAN DO IT
Chart the Stochastic Divergence
Number 1

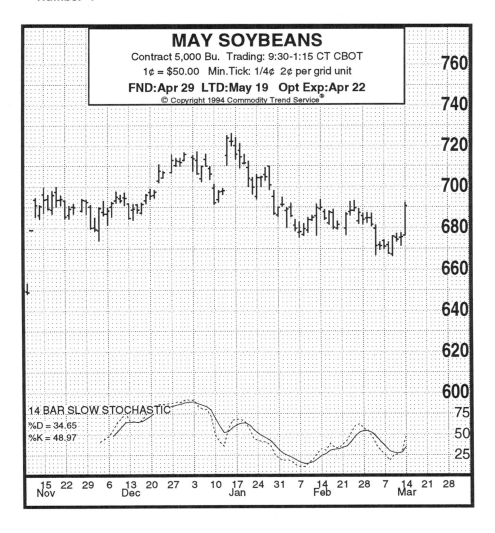

FIGURE 15.5   **ANSWER**
Stochastic Divergence
Number 1

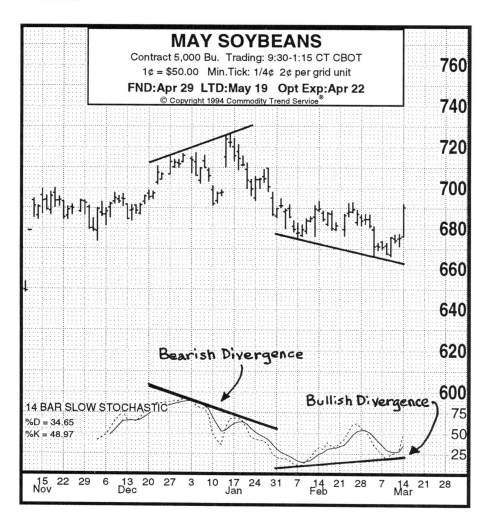

MAY SOYBEANS
Contract 5,000 Bu. Trading: 9:30-1:15 CT CBOT
1¢ = $50.00   Min.Tick: 1/4¢ 2¢ per grid unit
FND:Apr 29 LTD:May 19   Opt Exp:Apr 22
© Copyright 1994 Commodity Trend Service®

FIGURE 15.6 **YOU CAN DO IT**
Chart the Stochastic Divergence
Number 2

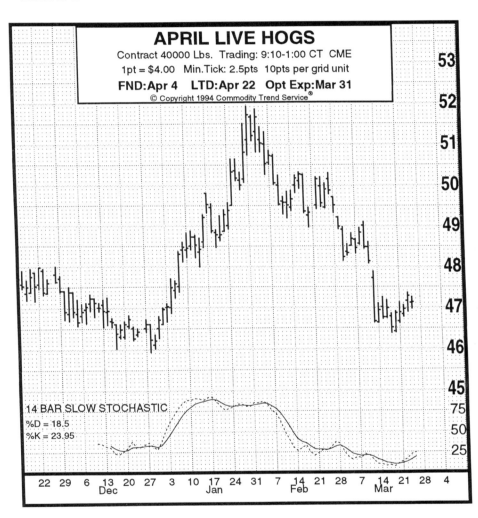

FIGURE 15.7   ANSWER
Stochastic Divergence
Number 2

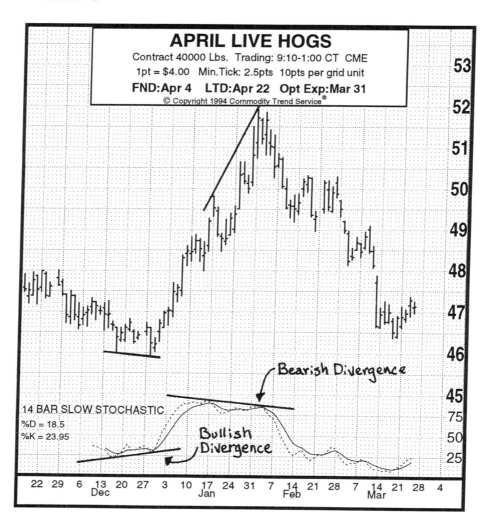

FIGURE 15.8   **YOU CAN DO IT**
Chart the Stochastic Divergence
Number 3

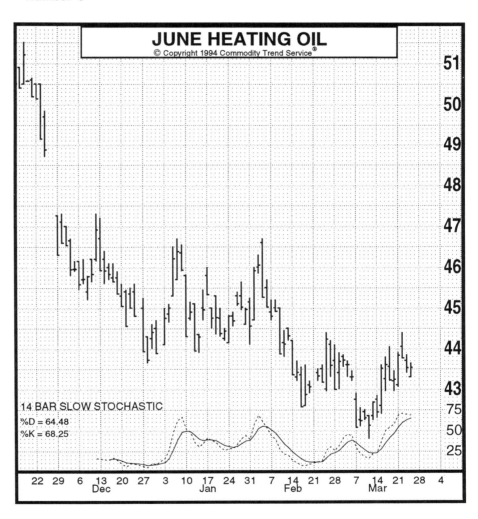

FIGURE 15.9   **ANSWER**
Stochastic Divergence
Number 3

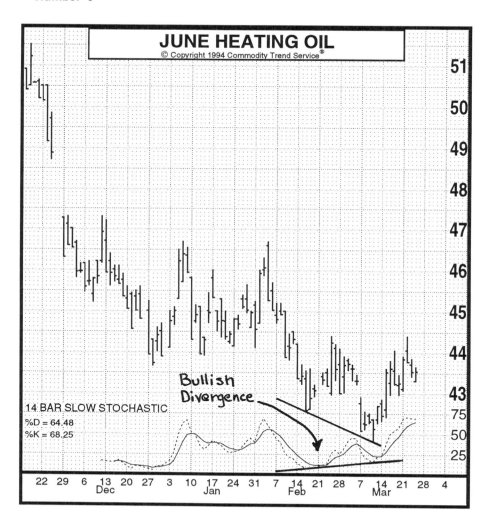

YOU CAN DO IT

In Figures 15.10–15.13, examine the stochastics chart near the last day. Indicate if you would go long, short or take no action. Remember, stochastics work best when they are in the overbought or oversold areas.

FIGURE 15.10   **YOU CAN DO IT**
Indicate Stochastic Buy/Sell Signals
Number 1

_____ **Long**   _____ **Short**   _____ **No Action**

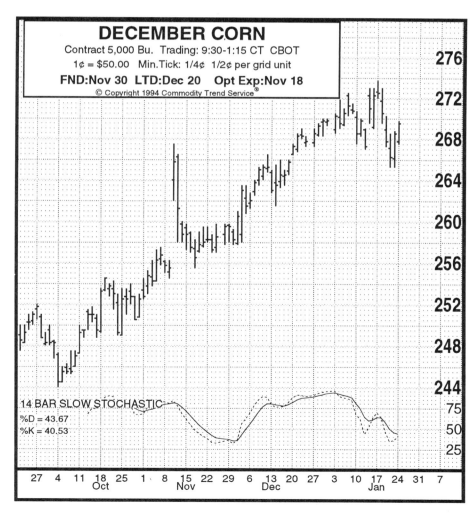

DECEMBER CORN
Contract 5,000 Bu. Trading: 9:30-1:15 CT CBOT
1¢ = $50.00   Min.Tick: 1/4¢ 1/2¢ per grid unit
FND:Nov 30 LTD:Dec 20   Opt Exp:Nov 18
© Copyright 1994 Commodity Trend Service®

14 BAR SLOW STOCHASTIC
%D = 43.67
%K = 40.53

FIGURE 15.11 **ANSWER**
Stochastic Buy/Sell Signals
Number 1

_____ **Long**   ✓ **Short**   _____ **No Action**

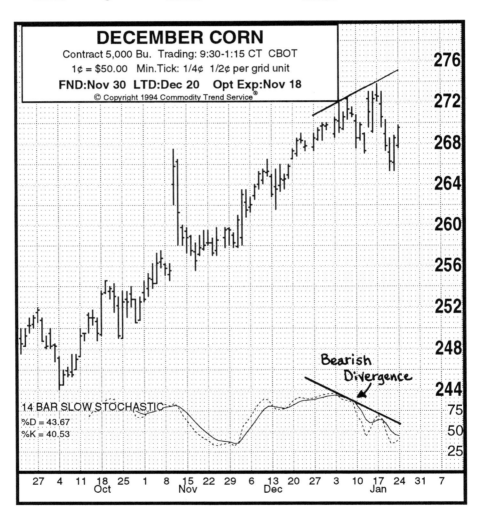

DECEMBER CORN
Contract 5,000 Bu. Trading: 9:30-1:15 CT CBOT
1¢ = $50.00   Min.Tick: 1/4¢ 1/2¢ per grid unit
FND:Nov 30 LTD:Dec 20   Opt Exp:Nov 18
© Copyright 1994 Commodity Trend Service®

14 BAR SLOW STOCHASTIC
%D = 43.67
%K = 40.53

Bearish Divergence

FIGURE 15.12 **YOU CAN DO IT**
Indicate Stochastic Buy/Sell Signals
Number 2

_____ **Long** _____ **Short** _____ **No Action**

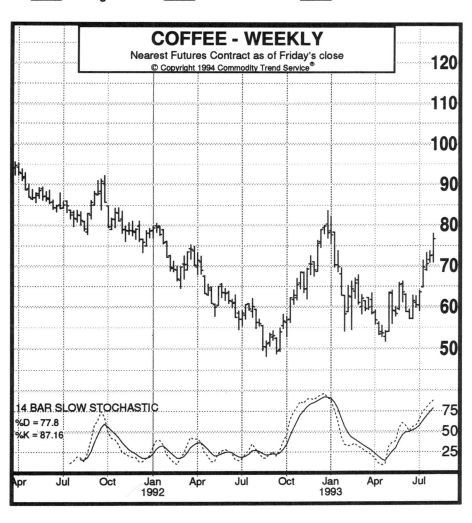

COFFEE - WEEKLY
Nearest Futures Contract as of Friday's close
© Copyright 1994 Commodity Trend Service®

14 BAR SLOW STOCHASTIC
%D = 77.8
%K = 87.16

FIGURE 15.13   **ANSWER**
Stochastic Buy/Sell Signals
Number 2

____ ✓ ____   **Long**   ____   **Short**   ____   **No Action**

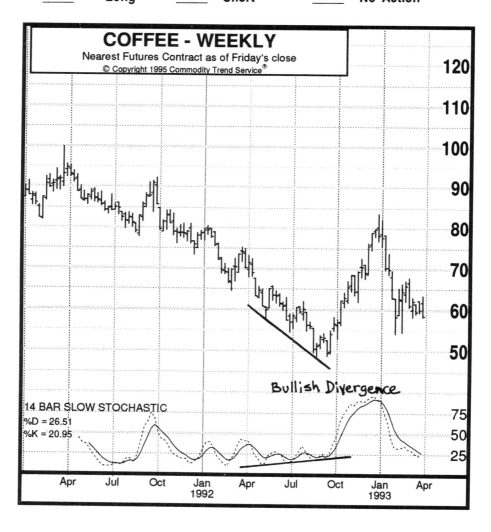

COFFEE - WEEKLY
Nearest Futures Contract as of Friday's close
© Copyright 1995 Commodity Trend Service®

Bullish Divergence

14 BAR SLOW STOCHASTIC
%D = 26.51
%K = 20.95

<table>
<tr><td>16</td><td># TAKING YOUR PROFITS— AVERAGE DIRECTIONAL MOVEMENT INDEX AND SEASONAL INDEX</td></tr>
</table>

For some individual traders, knowing when to get out of a profitable position is often more difficult than taking the original position. They worry about missing a big move. Professional traders, however, know when to let a position run and when to leave.

In this chapter, you will learn an important technique to capture big profits.

AVERAGE DIRECTIONAL MOVEMENT INDEX

The *average directional movement index* (ADX) is an indicator that can help you time profitable exit points when holding a futures position. ADX works best as a long-term indicator and, therefore, you will find it on weekly charts.

ADX Rule

Profitable traders who use ADX follow a very simple rule: *A climb by the ADX line above 40 followed by a downturn indicates an imminent end to the current trend.*

Using this rule, when the ADX line moves above 40 and then turns down, a trader should consider taking a profit. It does not matter if the primary trend is up or down. Once the ADX line turns down, it's a signal to exit and take a profit.

While an ADX signal can indicate the end of an existing trend, a reversal in the trend line is not always the next step. Instead, prices may enter a consolidation phase and move sideways for a period of time.

The average directional movement index is not helpful during sideways markets. During an extended consolidation period, an ADX line can slip below 20 and even approach ten on the scale. When the ADX approaches ten, a major move is usually about to take place. However, the ADX will not indicate which direction the move will go. You have to rely on other indicators for the probable direction of the next move.

In Figure 16.1, notice the profit-taking signals that the ADX line generates.

The average directional movement index can also be used as a filter, which is not the same as a prognosticator. A *prognosticator* gives an indication of a direction. A *filter* helps weed out erroneous signals.

You recall that both the RSI and the stochastic chart can indicate overbought or oversold positions for a long period of time, particularly during a strong trending market. To avoid selling or buying too soon, professional traders look at the ADX. As long as the ADX is rising, they stay with their positions. It acts as a filter to strain out false countertrend signals.

Always keep in mind that the ADX will not tell you when to reenter the market or take a position in the opposite direction. You will need other indicators to do that. Also, the ADX is not a price-sensitive indicator, because it is looking at a seven- or ten-week period. If you are interested in catching the absolute tops or bottoms, the ADX will be sluggish and will not give you the best signals. It is a far better indicator for long-term moves.

SEASONAL INDEX

To some extent, all commodity futures are influenced by annual seasonal cycles. As a case in point, grain markets are usually at seasonal lows around harvesttime when supply is at its highest. After that, prices tend to rise. Agri-

FIGURE 16.1   Example of the ADX

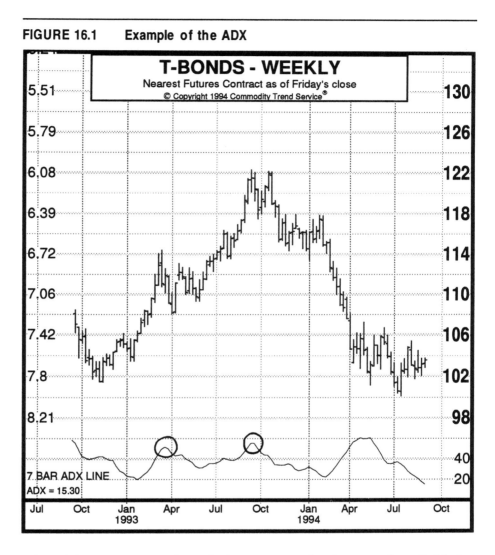

cultural futures are not the only instruments that have cycles. Gold, for example, often reaches a peak in January and then again in September.

Seasonal charts are computed based on the frequency of seasonal moves in the past. In Figure 16.2, the ADX and the seasonal index are placed on the same chart. By seeing both together, you have an opportunity to project major turning points.

FIGURE 16.2   Example of the ADX and the Seasonal Index

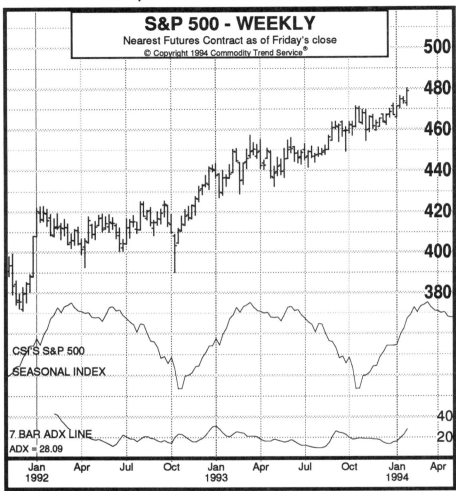

In the example shown in Figure 16.2, prices have moved up. However, the seasonal index is sloping downward. Next, we look at the ADX. It was above 40 but now it is moving down. If you were inclined to take a profit on the long position, you would be correct.

A seasonal index is just one more tool in your complete arsenal.

YOU CAN DO IT	Figures 16.3–16.8 are quick and easy exercises. In these examples, circle each time the ADX falls below 40. In addition, above each circle mark if you originally had been long or short. The purpose of these examples is to show that you can use the ADX to mark exit points for both long and short positions. Use the seasonal index (when appropriate) to help confirm your decision.

FIGURE 16.3   YOU CAN DO IT
Circle Exit Points (ADX Line)
Number 1

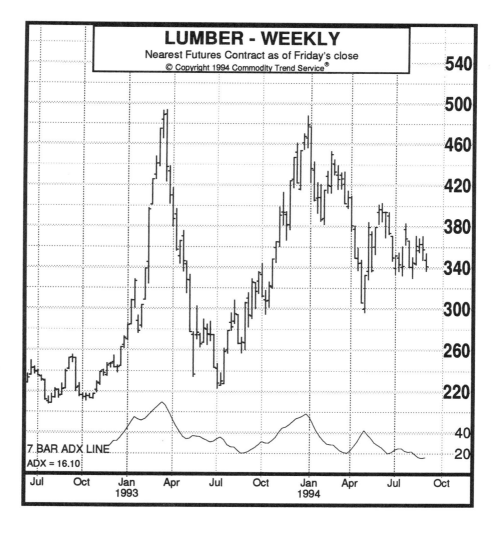

FIGURE 16.4   ANSWER
ADX Line
Number 1

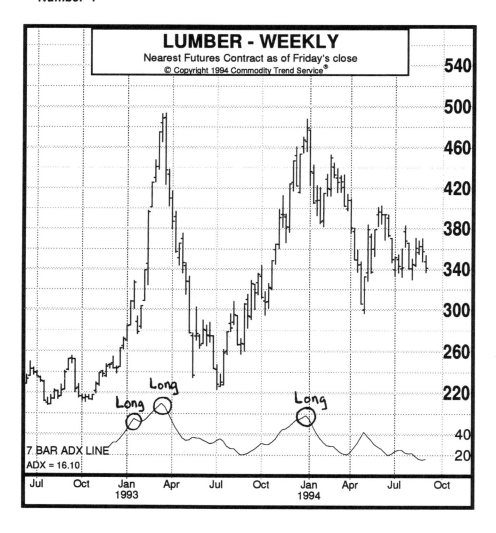

FIGURE 16.5   YOU CAN DO IT
Circle Exit Points (ADX Line)
Number 2

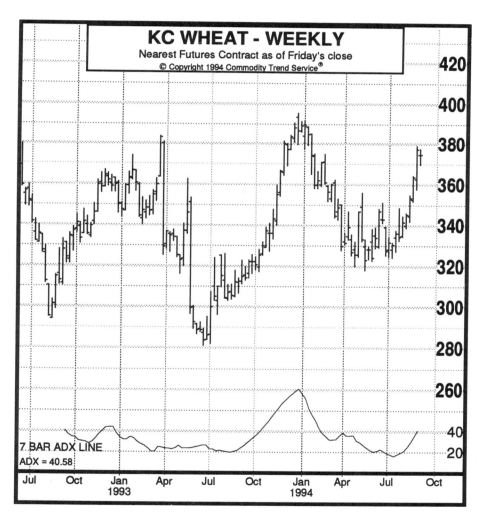

FIGURE 16.6   ANSWER
ADX Line
Number 2

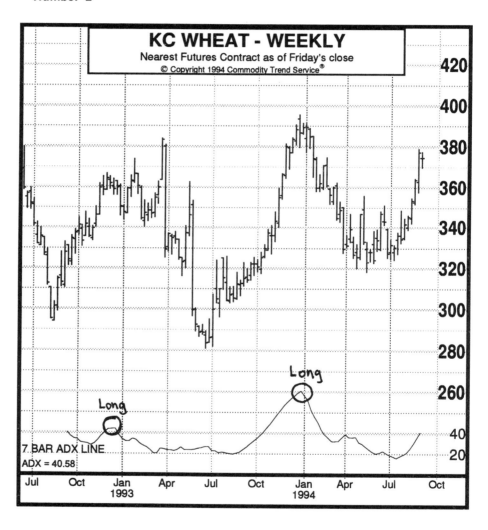

FIGURE 16.7   **YOU CAN DO IT**
Circle Exit Points (ADX and Seasonal Index)
Number 3

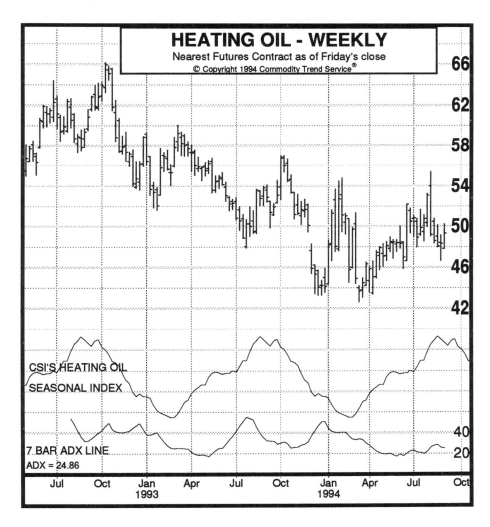

FIGURE 16.8   ANSWER
ADX and Seasonal Index
Number 3

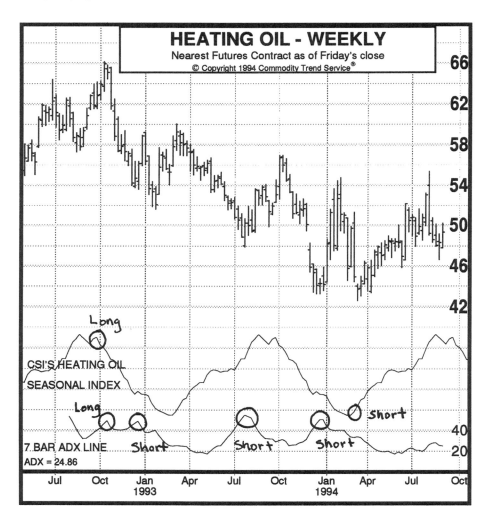

17

YOU CAN DO IT!— PUTTING IT ALL TOGETHER

You have covered a great deal of information in this book. Successful futures traders can make more than a million dollars using technical analysis, but it cannot be done overnight. Once again, practice makes perfect—and the more you use the tools, the more likely you'll be on your way to reaching and perhaps surpassing your financial goals that you desire.

PUTTING IT ALL TOGETHER

In this chapter, you will make five trading decisions. First, you will see the weekly chart of a specific futures instrument. Then you will be presented with the daily chart up to a certain date.

You'll be asked to decide whether to go long, short or take no action. In addition, jot down your rationale. Refer to specific indicators on the daily chart; use as many as you can. Make this real. The more you analyze, the more knowledge you'll acquire and the more skilled you will be to make big profits.

Figures 17.1 and 17.2 show a model response to a case study. Use them as guides to analyzing the examples in the rest of the chapter.

Figures 17.3–17.12 give the weekly and daily charts for five case studies. You will find the answers in Figures 17.13–17.17.

As you embark on your trading activities, think of the guidelines in Chapter 1. They can provide you with a sensible and sound approach to the markets.

Good luck and good trading!

FIGURE 17.1   Model Case Study (Daily Chart)

FIGURE 17.2   Model Case Study (Daily Chart)

_____ **Long**   ✓ **Short**   _____ **No Action**

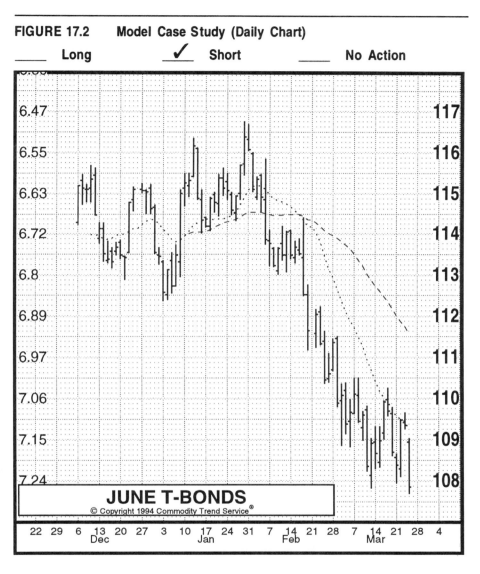

With the ADX line rising and the overall trend line being bearish on both the weekly and daily charts, going short would be a reasonable move.

FIGURE 17.3   Case Study (Weekly Chart)
                 Number 1

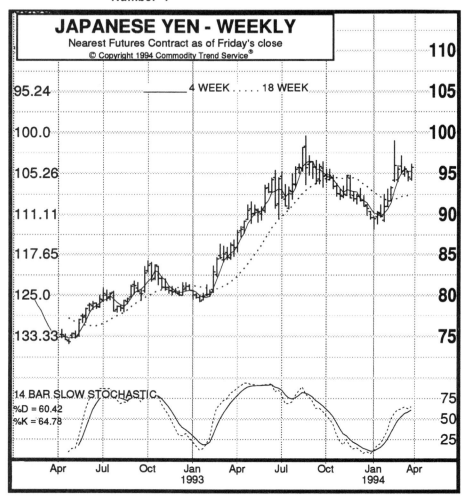

JAPANESE YEN - WEEKLY
Nearest Futures Contract as of Friday's close
© Copyright 1994 Commodity Trend Service®

FIGURE 17.4   Case Study (Daily Chart)
                 Number 1

_____ **Long**   _____ **Short**   _____ **No Action**

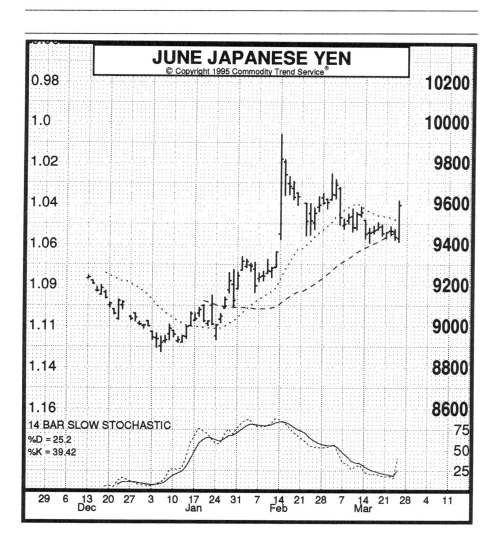

FIGURE 17.5   Case Study (Weekly Chart)
Number 2

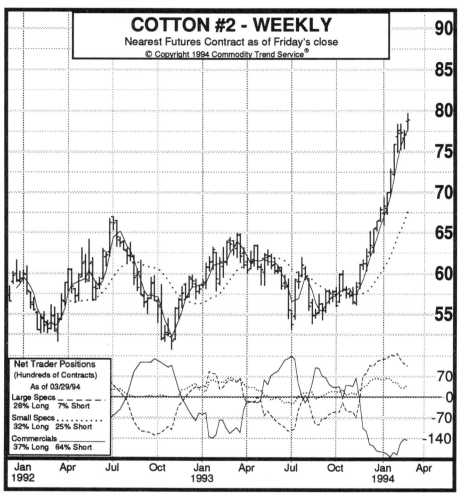

FIGURE 17.6   **Case Study (Daily Chart)**
                   Number 2

_____   **Long**   _____   **Short**   _____   **No Action**

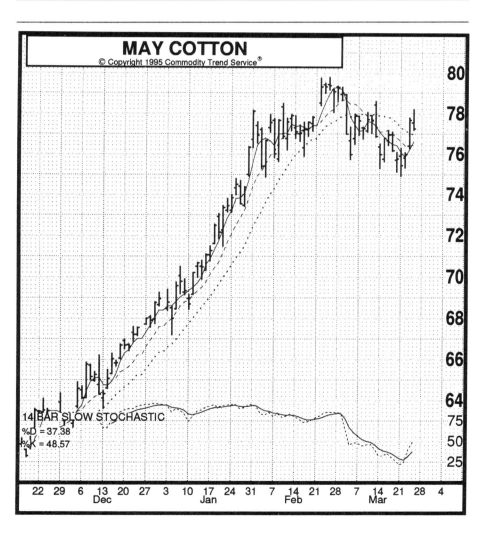

MAY COTTON
© Copyright 1995 Commodity Trend Service®

14 BAR SLOW STOCHASTIC
%D = 37.38
%K = 48.57

FIGURE 17.7   Case Study (Weekly Chart)
                  Number 3

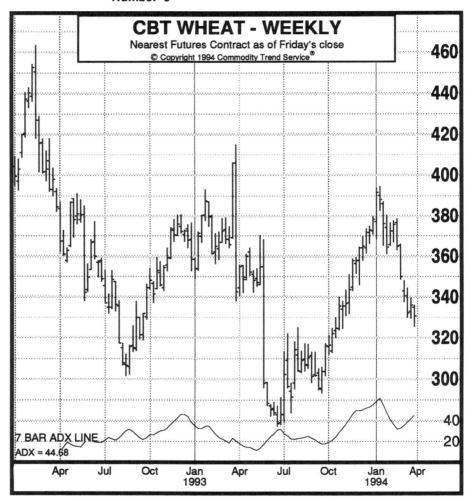

FIGURE 17.8   Case Study (Daily Chart)
                     Number 3

_____   **Long**   _____   **Short**   _____   **No Action**

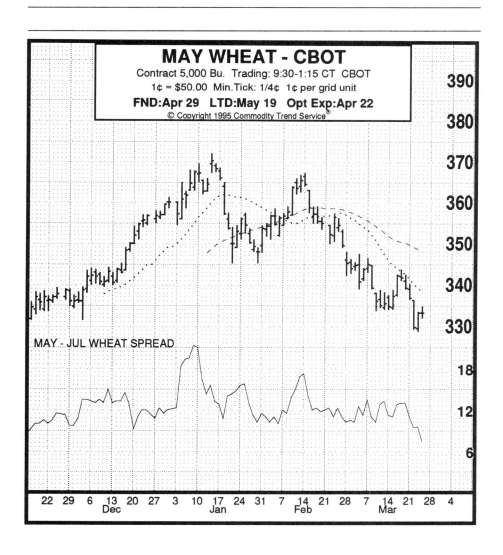

FIGURE 17.9   Case Study (Weekly Chart)
                      Number 4

FIGURE 17.10   Case Study (Daily Chart)
                Number 4

_____ Long   _____ Short   _____ No Action

FIGURE 17.11   Case Study (Weekly Chart)
                   Number 5

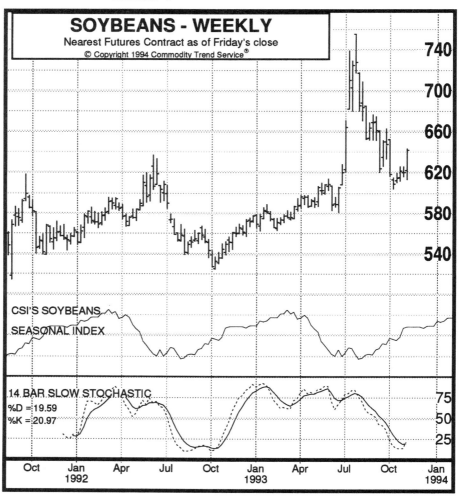

FIGURE 17.12   Case Study (Daily Chart)
                Number 5

_____ **Long**   _____ **Short**   _____ **No Action**

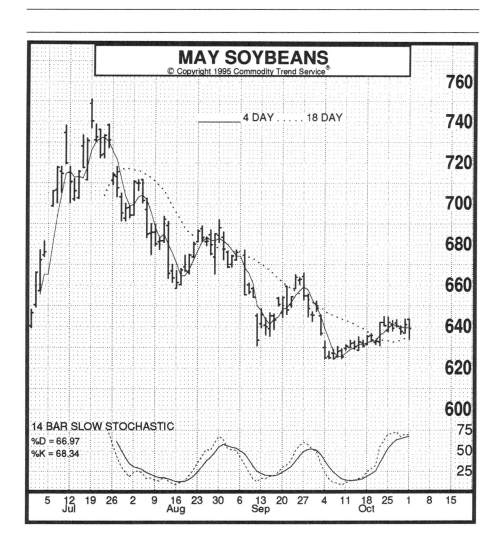

FIGURE 17.13   Answer: Case Study
Number 1

✓ _____ Long   _____ Short   _____ No Action

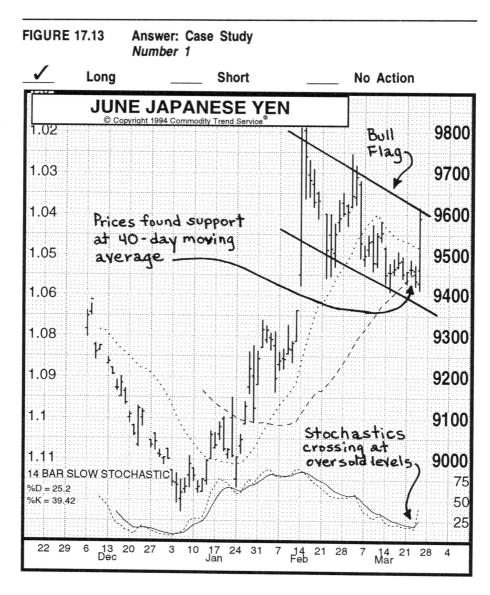

The primary trend, as indicated by the weekly chart, is definitely up. All key moving averages are in a bullish alignment. Notice the bull flag forming just above the 40-day moving average. Finally, bottoming daily stochastics provided an excellent timing signal for going long. Eight weeks later, prices traded up to 99.40. A top trader could have made nearly $3,750 per contract.

FIGURE 17.14   Answer: Case Study
                   Number 2

✓ Long   _____ Short   _____ No Action

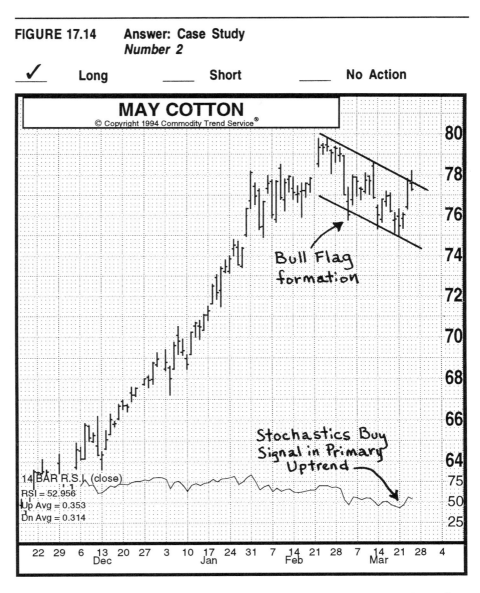

Despite recent losses in March, the primary trend is bullish, with prices above the 18-week moving average on the weekly chart. Notice also that commercials moved out of short positions in February and March. On the daily chart, a bull flag and bottoming stochastics can help you time a long position. A few weeks later, the market traded at 86 cents. By taking a long position, you could have made over $4,000 per contract.

FIGURE 17.15   **Answer: Case Study**
                      Number 3

_____ Long   ✓ Short   _____ No Action

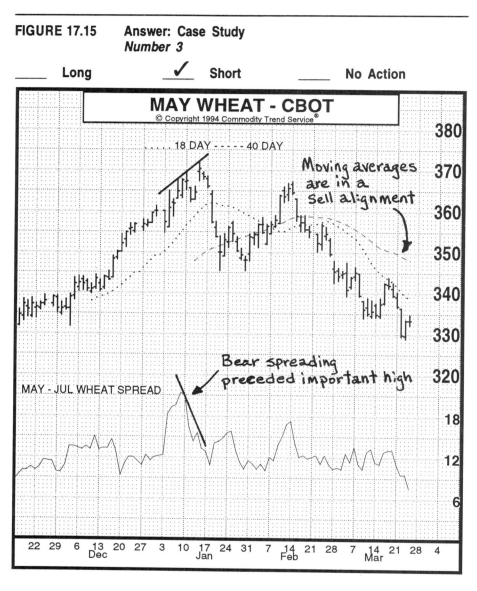

Notice, on the weekly chart, the clear pattern of lower intermediate-term highs (Feb. 1992, April 1993 and Jan. 1994) and lower intermediate-term lows (Aug. 1992 and June 1993). The rising weekly ADX line confirms the strength of the trend. Bear spreading and falling moving averages on the daily chart are also confirming signals. Taking a short position here would be appropriate. Prices eventually dropped to the 313 area.

FIGURE 17.16   Answer: Case Study Number 4

✓ ___ Long   ___ Short   ___ No Action

MAY SILVER - COMEX
© Copyright 1994 Commodity Trend Service®

40 DAY MA

Stochastics Buy Signal in Uptrend

14 BAR SLOW STOCHASTIC
%D = 39.28
%K = 43.46

In 1993 and 1994, we had higher highs and higher lows. The rising ADX line indicated the upside momentum was still in charge. Turning to the daily chart, notice how the uptrend remained intact. Furthermore, stochastics completed a downward cycle, thus setting up a very strong buy signal. Just a few weeks later, silver exploded to 5.80.

**FIGURE 17.17   Answer: Case Study
                    Number 5**

✓____ Long   ____ Short   ____ No Action

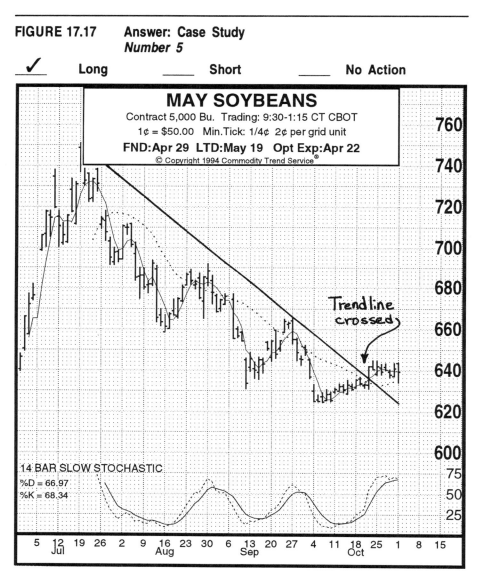

On the weekly chart, there was a bullish trend line from October 1992 through
the end of the chart. Also in the third quarter of 1993, the CSI seasonal index
and the weekly stochastics were approaching lows, thus pointing to higher
prices. On the daily chart, prices moved lower from July, but moved up in late
October. Stochastics and moving average crossovers indicate it was time to go
long again—in the direction of the primary trend. In the next 12 weeks, prices
rallied to over $7.00 a bushel. By going long, you could have made over
$3,000 a contract.

GLOSSARY

analysis, fundamental   Market research based on supply and demand (that a scarcity of a commodity should result in a higher average price level)

analysis, technical   The study of market action, primarily through the use of charts, to anticipate price trends

average   The mean or middle value in a series of numbers

average, moving   A technical indicator that smooths daily closing prices

cash market   Also known as the *actual* or *spot market*. This is where commodities are transacted on a negotiated basis and where the commodity physically trades hands, e.g., from a farmer to a food processor.

channel   A chart formation that occurs when prices fluctuate within a discernible pattern that can be drawn by two parallel lines

channel, trendless   A chart formation in which a channel travels sideways; this formation is also called a *congestion area.*

confirmation   When prices move up rapidly along with heavy volume

congestion areas   See *channel, trendless*

crossover   A pattern in which different moving averages cross over one another

cycle   A repetitive sequence of events; in commodities, most common cycles are long term (two to ten years), seasonal (one year) or primary or intermediate (two to six months).

delivery, forward   When a futures contract specifies immediate delivery at a time set in the future

distribution   When investors sell off their positions

divergence   A price pattern that occurs when a price line and an oscillator line begin to diverge and move in opposite directions; when prices increase, but volume has decreased

divergence, bearish   A pattern in which the price trend line moves upward, yet the relative strength index chart is moving down

divergence, bullish   A pattern in which the price trend line moves downward, yet the relative strength index chart is moving up

double bottom   Price pattern that occurs in a *W* pattern

double top   Price pattern that occurs in an *M* pattern

downtick   Downward price change

downtrend   A pattern of lower price highs and lower price lows

equity   Value in an account

failure swing   When the relative strength index's failure to make a new high is followed by a drop below its previous low

flag   A small parallelogram that often forms after a rapid price move

flag, bear   Countertrend formation found after a rapid price move in a downtrend

flag, bull   Countertrend price move forming after a dynamic advance

floor broker   One who executives trades for others

futures contract   A pair of promises—one, to deliver the underlying commodity, and the other, to pay for it

gap   Price range on a chart where no actual trading has taken place

gap, breakaway   A gap that occurs at the end of a sideways consolidation pattern, indicating the beginning of a significant price move

gap, common   Price area on a chart where no trading occurred

gap, exhaustion   A gap that occurs within a couple of days of a climax top or bottom, indicating a trend that has run out of steam

gap, measuring   A gap that occurs after a trend has been established

indicator   A tool used to detect the strength or weakness of a trend

indicator, leading   A tool that can precede market movement (i.e., cash basis and spreads)

indicator, trailing   A tool that follows the market only (i.e., moving averages)

line, resistance   The higher line in a channel that occurs when there are more sellers than buyers, signaling a price retreat

line, support   The lower line in a channel that occurs when there is sufficient buying interest to overcome selling pressure

local   A floor trader who trades for his or her own account

long   A position that will profit from rising prices

margin   An investor's "good faith" deposit in a futures transaction

margin, house   The amount of money an investor is required to deposit, established by an individual firm, that exceeds the deposit required by the exchange

margin, maintenance   Money required to maintain a losing position, typically 25 percent lower than initial

margin, original or initial   The sum of money an investor is required to deposit—ranges from 2 percent to 10 percent of the contract's value

margin call, variance or maintenance   When a member firm requests additional funds because the margin has been reduced to the maintenance margin

market sentiment   A reflection of how bullish a universe of professional trades are on a particular future product during a given time

marking to the market   When money is credited to or debited from an account based on the amount the contract has moved during the day

momentum   The rate of change of prices over a given period, as opposed to the actual prices themselves

net trader position   The result of subtracting short and long holdings of a particular group of traders (i.e., commercials, small and large speculators)

open interest   The total number of outstanding contracts held at the end of the day; total number of all longs or shorts, but not both

overbought   A market condition resulting from excessive speculative buying

oversold   A condition resulting from excessive selling

pattern, continuation   A sideways price formation that represents a pause in a major trend

pattern, reversal   A formation that indicates a trend is about to make a significant change in direction

pennants   Small triangular formations that often form after a rapid price move

position, offset   To liquidate an existing position

relative strength index   A momentum indicator derived from the daily net changes of closing prices

reversal   A signal that a trend has reversed

reversal day   A trading day in which a run-up of prices reaches a new high in one day, only to fall below the lower level established on the previous day

reversal, island   A pattern in which a cluster of days stands apart from the rest of the prices around them

short   A position that profits from falling prices

smart money   Investments by commodity traders who are closely involved with the commodity and trading fundamentals

spread   The purchase and sale of two contracts in the same commodity

spread, bear   The short sale of a nearby month and the taking of a long position on a distant month

spread, bull   A transaction in which the trader purchases a nearby contract and goes short on the distant contract

stage, public part   A market phase featuring extreme bullishness; similar to the Dow theories distribution phase

stage, trend-following   Market phase resulting in a large price move. Technical, trend-following traders can make fortunes during this phase.

stochastics   momentum; explained through a future's daily high, low and closing prices

tick   Smallest price change

translation   When most of the highs within a cycle occur to the right or the left of the midpoint

translation, left   In a bear market, when the apex of a cycle leans to the left of the midpoint

translation, right   In a bull market, when the crest leans to the right because the highs are to the right of the cycle's midpoint.

trend, minor   A price move lasting from a few days to a few weeks

trend, primary   A trend lasting greater than six months

trend, secondary   A price move lasting from a few weeks to a few months

trend line   A line connecting two or more highs (lows)

triangles   Patterns that form when short-term uptrend and downtrend lines intersect

uptick   Upward price change

uptrend   A pattern of rising peaks and valleys, with each successive high and low being higher than the previous respective peak or valley

volume   The total number of contracts traded during the day; total number of "buys" or "sells," but not both

INDEX

ABOUT THE AUTHOR

Nathan J. Sambul is a leading financial futures, commodities and options educator. For the past 25 years, he has written articles, produced videotapes and taught hundreds of investors and brokers how to get the highest investment returns. Mr. Sambul began his career on Wall Street as a registered representative and manager of a major corporate communication department.